Getting Your Money's Worth from Training and Development

PARTICIPANTS

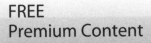

FREE Premium Content	Pfeiffer® An Imprint of WILEY
This book includes premium content that can be accessed from our Web site when you register at **www.pfeiffer.com/go/forthill** using the password *professional*.	

Checklist for Participants

 **Checklist**

Here are the actions you need to take to be sure you get your money's worth from training and development. Check them off as you complete them.

	Done	Date	Key Actions
PREPARE	☐	_____	Complete the WIIFM Form.
	☐	_____	Share and discuss with your manager.
	☐	_____	List the preparatory work assignments below and complete them:
	☐	_____	1. _____
	☐	_____	2. _____
	☐	_____	3. _____
ATTEND	☐	_____	Focus on learning and reflection; minimize interruptions.
	☐	_____	Try new and different behaviors or ways of interacting.
	☐	_____	Truly connect with others in the program.
	☐	_____	Connect course material to what you already know and have experienced.
	☐	_____	Speak up or challenge appropriately to make sure you get value.
	☐	_____	Set clear, compelling, and challenging goals to improve your performance.
APPLY	☐	_____	Meet with your manager to recap and secure support.
	☐	_____	Take first action within three days.
	☐	_____	Stop, reflect, and journal your progress at least five times (online or on paper).
	☐	_____	Update 1
	☐	_____	Update 2
	☐	_____	Update 3
	☐	_____	Update 4
	☐	_____	Update 5
	☐	_____	Ask advisors for feedback and coaching.
	☐	_____	Summarize—in writing—your achievements.
	☐	_____	Figure out—and write down—your next most important development challenge.
	☐	_____	Share your summary and future plans with your manager.

Getting Your Money's Worth from Training and Development

A Guide to Breakthrough
Learning for Participants

Andrew McK. Jefferson

Roy V.H. Pollock

Calhoun W. Wick

Pfeiffer

A Wiley Imprint
www.pfeiffer.com

Published by Pfeiffer
A Wiley Imprint
989 Market Street, San Francisco, CA 94103-1741
www.pfeiffer.com

For additional copies/bulk purchases of this book in the U.S. please contact 800-274-4434.

Pfeiffer books and products are available through most bookstores. To contact Pfeiffer directly call our Customer Care Department within the U.S. at 800-274-4434, outside the U.S. at 317-572-3985, fax 317-572-4002, or visit www.pfeiffer.com.

Pfeiffer also publishes its books in a variety of electronic formats. Some content that appears in print may not be available in electronic books.

ISBN 978-0-470-41112-4

Acquiring Editor: Matthew Davis
Marketing Manager: Brian Grimm
Production Editor: Michael Kay
Editor: Rebecca Taff
Manufacturing Supervisor: Becky Morgan
Editorial Assistant: Lindsay Morton
Interior Composition: Stan Shoptaugh
Illustrations: Lotus Art

Printed in the United States of America
Printing   10 9 8 7 6 5 4 3 2 1

Contents

List of Inserts

A Guide to Breakthrough Learning for Participants

Contents of the Website

Results Readiness Scorecards

Job Aids

More Frequently Asked Questions

More "Who Says So?"

Case Studies

More Sample Worksheets

Additional Tips and Guides

Learn More

A Guide to Breakthrough Learning for Participants

How to Use This Book

This book is a "How-To" guide. It provides succinct, practical, proven advice on how to get the most from training and development. It is short because it is not that hard to get a big return from training and development—provided you do the necessary work. Like so many other things in life, you get out what you put in. No investment, no return.

To save you time, we have separated the "need to know" from the "nice to know." What you must do to get your money's worth from training is explained in this typeface on the white pages. If you are by nature a driver, somebody who just likes to "get 'er done," or if you are short of time right now, just read the non-shaded pages and complete the ✏️ Do It Now worksheets. Use the checklist provided inside the front cover to keep track.

If you are by nature analytical, curious about the theory and data behind the recommendations, or skeptical about the advice in self-help books, then read the ⬆️ Who Says So? sections in the sans-serif typeface on a gray background. Optional 💭 Think About It exercises and the answers to Frequently Asked Questions ❓ FAQs are also set off on gray backgrounds. There are completed examples of the worksheets in the appendix.

The flip side of this book is advice to your manager—what he or she can do to help you and, at the same time, be sure your company and department get *their* money's worth. Because you may one day be—or perhaps already are—a manager of others, we encourage you to look through the advice to managers as well.

Introduction to the Guide for Participants

Think about how good it feels to be recognized for a job well done, to earn a raise, win a promotion, or be asked to lead an important project. How do you get more of those good things?

You get better at what you do.

One important way to improve your performance is to attend training and development programs that enhance your knowledge and skills. You are holding a copy of this book because you are scheduled to attend such a program. It might be a program you signed up for, one that is required for your job, or one that was recommended to help advance your career. You might be enthusiastic about attending, apprehensive, or even irritated. It doesn't matter. You need to make the most of it. The program is going to consume your time and your employer's money. You can choose to waste it or to extract maximum value.

This book will show you how to get the most from training and development programs, take responsibility for your personal development, improve your performance, and make more good things come your way. Completing the worksheets in this guide will help ensure that you—and your employer—get your money's worth.

So What?

Why should you care, especially if you did not choose to attend?

Because what you do with what you are taught will help or hurt your career. To get ahead, you need to show that you can continue to learn and grow in your job, that investing in you pays a return. It would be a mistake to gain a reputation as someone who is inflexible or uncoachable or who wastes time and company resources.

> *Your company invests in training and development*
> *to help you improve your performance.*
> *Show that you are a good investment.*

Everyone Can Improve

No matter how good you are, you can still get better. The world's top performers in every field—business, athletics, engineering, arts—never stop trying to improve. Neither should you. It is a competitive world. You need to get better or you'll get left behind.

> *Even if you are on the right track, you'll*
> *get run over if you just stand there.*
> —Will Rogers

Use Worksheet 1.1 to identify your three best opportunities to improve your performance.

Standing Still Is Not an Option

The fact is, you have no choice: you have to show improvement after the program you are scheduled to attend.

"Bad news, Gilchrist—somehow you've come to someone's attention."

Why? First, because even if you don't, others will. As they become more valuable, you will become relatively less valuable.

Second, because people will know you went. Your manager, your peers, and your direct reports will notice your absence. You may have asked them to provide feedback. Someone had to cover for you while you were out.

The mere fact that you attended a training program causes their expectations to go up. If their expectations go up, but your performance doesn't change, then—relatively—you're *less* effective than you were before (Figure 1.1).

> *Whenever you attend a training program, expectations go up.*

WORKSHEET 1.1
Opportunities for Improvement

Do It Now

Instructions: List three things that, if you could do them faster, better, or more effectively, would make you even more valuable than you are today:

1. _____
   _____

2. _____
   _____

3. _____
   _____

Figure 1.1

Expectations Go Up After a Training Program.
If Your Performance Remains the Same, You Will Fall Behind.

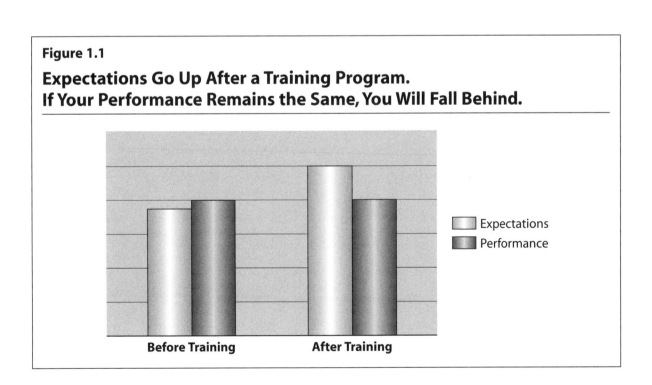

It's Up to You

You determine whether or not training pays off. If you don't improve, you have no one to blame but yourself. Even if the program isn't the greatest, you can still learn something; even if your manager does not provide the support he or she should, you can still do something. You are not a victim. Your company is providing the opportunity; it's up to you to get your money's worth.

> *"All development is ultimately self-development."*
> —Peter Drucker

The Three Keys to Getting Your Money's Worth as a Participant

To get your money's worth from your upcoming training and development opportunity:

1. Get Ready

2. Get Engaged

3. Get Results

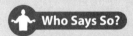 **Who Says So?** *You Need to Get Ready*

Preparing ahead helps you get more out of the program; it increases your return on investment.

There is clear evidence that those who meet with their managers prior to a training program create learning intentionality that pays off as greater improvement compared to those who attend the same program but don't meet with their managers beforehand (Brinkerhoff & Apking, 2001, p. 92).

Likewise, learning research has shown that once we decide that we want to learn something, our brains are subconsciously alerted to attend to information about the topic. When we encounter data relevant to what we have decided we want to learn, the brain spends more time processing it than processing unrelated facts. The additional processing makes the information easier to remember and use subsequently. Deciding what you want to learn, in effect, makes it easier to learn it.

Finally, well-designed training programs usually include preparation—reading, assessments, or other assignments (sometimes referred to as pre-work) that will be used during the training itself. Completing these assignments is essential to participate fully in the program. Moreover, research confirms their importance. Recall is greatly improved by "spaced learning," that is, revisiting the same topic more than once with an interval between (Dempster, 1989; Medina, 2008, p. 100). You'll master the material faster and more completely if you encounter it twice, once in the preparatory work and again in the program itself.

1. Get Ready

Getting prepared is one of the most important things you can do to get value from a training program (see "Who Says So?", p. 9). The three steps to getting ready are:

☐ Get clear about what YOU want.

☐ Get your manager's agreement

☐ Get the preparation done.

"Please, Ms. Sweeney, may I ask where you're going with all this?"

Get Clear About What YOU Want

If you don't know what you want to get out of a learning experience, you will get less than you could have. Whether you signed up for this program voluntarily or whether it is a command performance, you'll get a better return on your investment if you figure out: "What's in it for me?" (WIIFM). To do so, complete Worksheet 1.2 WIIFM.

The WIIFM for each person, even though they are attending the same program, is different. Your personal WIIFM depends on your job responsibilities, career goals, interests, experience and developmental needs.

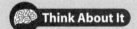 **Think About It**   *Two Learners*

Two learners arrive at the same program.

One knows exactly what she wants to get out of it. The other arrives with just a vague idea of what the program is about.

Who is likely to come away with greater value?

What is the implication for you?

No one can define your WIIFM for you. The objectives for the program as a whole aren't specific enough to answer the WIIFM question for you or to guide your personal learning. So you'll benefit by taking a few minutes to become clear about what you, personally, want in return for the time you will be investing.

WORKSHEET 1.2
WIIFM for Participants

Your Name: _____

Name of Program: _____   Date of Program: _____

Instructions for Participants

1. In the first column of the row labeled "Your Input," write two to five bullet points that summarize the key deliverables for your unit. (See the completed examples in the appendix.) Why does your group exist? How does it create value for the business? This step is key; training and development must ultimately support the business's or organization's objectives.

2. In the box in column 2, write the specific results for which you, personally, are accountable. Ideally, these should be top of mind and mesh exactly with your annual performance goals, but they are worth revisiting.

3. In column 3, list what would help you do your current job better or prepare you for next step in your career. What are the top performers in your field able to do better than you can currently? What will get you recognized, rewarded, promoted?

4. Once you are clear about your best personal opportunities, look at the course description and objectives. What does it cover? What does it promise? [If you don't know, find out.] Note these in column 4.

5. Now put what you have written in columns 3 and 4 together to fill in the box in column 5.

6. Schedule a time to review your completed WIIFM Worksheet with your manager.

Instructions for Managers

1. Review your direct report's input. Compare this with your views (preferably with what you wrote on Worksheet 2.2, which you completed independently).

2. Discuss areas of agreement or differences of opinion with your direct report.

3. Use the results and your notes to formulate a formal or informal "learning contract."

	1. Most important deliverables of my business/ organizational unit	2. Most important results for which I am personally responsible	3. New or improved skills/knowledge that would help me deliver better results	4. Objectives covered in the training or development program	5. Therefore, what I want to get out of it (be able to do better or differently)
Your Input					
Your Manager's Review	☐ Agree as written ☐ See edits ☐ Let's discuss	☐ Agree as written ☐ See edits ☐ Let's discuss	☐ Agree as written ☐ See edits ☐ Let's discuss	☐ Agree as written ☐ See edits ☐ Let's discuss	☐ Agree as written ☐ See edits ☐ Let's discuss
Comments:					

Do It Now

FAQs   *What If the Course Has No Apparent Value for Me?*

Suppose that after reviewing the content of the program you are scheduled to attend, you cannot see any-thing in the course that is of value to you. You have a couple of choices: If the program is voluntary, then you may decide not to go, using the time and money saved to attend a program with a be-tter payoff for you personally.

If the training is required, you could try to talk your way out it. That may not be the best option, because it is unlikely to succeed ("required" means you have to do it, after all) and it may earn you a reputation as uncooperative, a know it all, or intransigent.

But if the program really seems to be a waste of time because it is unrelated to your job, you have taken it before, or you are considered an expert in the area, then talk to your manager about options. She/he should be as interested as you are in seeing that your time is used well and may be willing to question the value of such required training with the management team.

Another option is to figure out something you can gain from the required training, even if it is not in your "sweet spot." For example, you could use the opportunity to brush up on old skills or add details you might have forgotten. If it is a classroom session, you can use it to practice your interpersonal skills; network with people from other areas or lines of business; add value by teaching others; or watch the instructors to polish your presentation skills.

In short, you can always learn something of value from a required training program, even if it may not be what the designers had in mind.

Get Your Manager's Agreement

Once you are clear on what <u>you</u> want to get out of the training, share it with your manager. Take the completed WIIFM form (Worksheet 1.2) to your manager for review. *Do not skip this step!*

> *Meeting with your manager before a program positively impacts the outcome and how your efforts are perceived.*

Meeting with your manager before you go to a training program has many benefits. For one thing, it is a great opportunity to gain additional feedback on your performance and some coaching on how you can improve and get ahead. If you want to increase your chances for promotion and additional responsibility, you need to know where your manager thinks you can enhance your performance.

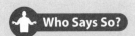 **Who Says So?** *You Should Meet with Your Manager*

Your manager is the gatekeeper for your access to raises, promotions, and further developmental opportunities. His/her perceptions of your performance and of your ability to learn and develop significantly impact your career. You need your manager's support to spend time developing your skills; she or he can provide you stretch assignments and other opportunities for growth.

So meeting with your manager in advance of training just makes good sense. You want to be confident that you and your manager are in agreement about your key developmental needs and opportunities.

There is also good evidence that meeting with your manager ahead of training yields better results. For example, Brinkerhoff and Montesino (1995) found that participants who had discussions with their managers before and after training achieved significantly higher levels of skill application than people in the same programs who did not have these conversations. Corporate trainers also recognize the importance of a pre-course meeting. They rated a before-training meeting with managers as having greater impact on learning transfer than their own role during the training! (Broad & Newstrom, 1992, p. 53)

Another reason to meet with your manager is that you will need his or her support and approval to spend time improving your skills. It is far better to secure these in advance, and to be sure you are working on areas with the biggest potential payback, than to discover later that your manager had a different set of priorities in mind.

 **Think About It**   *Why Does a Discussion with Your Manager Help?*

People who discuss an upcoming program with their manager beforehand are much more likely to follow-through, transfer, and apply what they learn.

Why? What are the implications for you?

Write It Down

Make notes of your discussion with your manager. When you write down what you plan to do, you are more likely to do it (Allen, p. 21). If your relationship with your manager is fairly formal, complete and sign the Learning Contract (Worksheet 1.3) at the end of your meeting.

WORKSHEET 1.3
Learning Contract

 **Do It Now**

YOUR COMMITMENT

In order to maximize the value of my learning and development in the upcoming _____
_____ program, I agree to:

☐ Complete all required pre-course reading and other assignments
☐ Attend and be actively engaged in all sessions
☐ Develop goals for applying what I learned to my work
☐ Execute a follow-through plan that improves my performance
☐ Report the results
☐ Share highlights and insights with my co-workers
☐ Other_____

Specifically, I will focus on _____ during the program in order to improve my _____
_____ afterward.

Signed: _____

Date: _____

MANAGER'S AGREEMENT

As the manager of the employee above, I agree to:

1. Attend and participate in any advance briefing sessions for supervisors.

2. Meet with my direct report before the program to discuss the most important developmental opportunities the training provides.

3. Release my direct report from sufficient work assignments that he/she has time to complete the preparation for the training and attend all the sessions.

4. Minimize interruptions during the training.

5. Meet again after the program to discuss the highlights of the session and provide coaching and support to mutually explore opportunities for application.

6. Model the desired behaviors.

7. Provide encouragement, support, and reinforcement for efforts to apply the training.

8. Provide specific opportunities for my direct report to practice the new behaviors and skills.

9. Provide suggestions for continued development.

Our post-course follow-up meeting is scheduled for: _____

Signed: _____

Date: _____

FAQs   *What If My Manager Is Too Busy to Meet with Me?*

Everyone in business is busy these days, managers especially so. Most managers make time to meet with their direct reports, despite their heavy workloads. But it may be that your manager is truly under pressure to meet a near-term deadline. Or it may be that your manager prefers to communicate in writing or by telephone. It may be that he/she does not consider this a priority. In any case, send your completed WIIFM Worksheet to your manager. Ask for a short teleconference or written feedback, depending on your manager's needs and preferences.

If your manager is still too busy to provide you with input prior to the program, that is unfortunate. You, your manager, and the business are missing an opportunity. But do not let your manager's failure stand in the way of your own development and advancement. Find another advisor, such as a manager you respect, a high-performing colleague, someone in HR. Seek an advisor who knows your performance and business role well enough to give you sound advice and who cares enough about your success to give you constructive feedback—the good news as well as the bad—to help you focus your energy and efforts.

If your relationship with your manager is more informal, you should still commemorate the meeting and your commitments in a memo or email immediately afterward. Worksheet 1.4 provides a suggested format.

Schedule the Follow-Up Meeting

Finally, schedule a time to meet with your manager soon after you return from the program. Do this as part of the pre-training discussion; it will pay dividends later.

Get the Pre-Assigned Work Done

Most programs—especially those of greater substance or longer duration—require some sort of preparation. Preparation might include readings, self-evaluations, online exercises, feedback instruments, or other experiences that the designers feel are critical for you to get the greatest value from your time in the program itself. Preparation is an integral part of the complete learning experience and vital to your success.

> *Make the time and do the pre-course work.*

As busy as you are these days, it is tempting to save a few hours by skipping the preparation or leaving it to the last minute, but that is false economy. You may well save a couple of hours before the program, only to waste a great deal more than that in the course by being inadequately prepared.

WORKSHEET 1.4
Learning Memorandum

 **Do It Now**

Dear _____ ,

Thank you for meeting with me today to discuss the upcoming _____
Program.

We agreed that the most important thing for me to focus on during the course was _____
_____ in order to improve my performance in the area of
_____ .

You agreed to make sure that I had the time to do the assignments, attend the program
with minimum interruptions, and have opportunities to practice my new skills / knowledge
afterward. You also agreed to provide coaching so that I can benefit from your expertise
and experience.

We scheduled a post-course follow-up meeting on _____ at _____ ,
at which I will share my reactions to the program, the most important insights, and my
specific goals for achievement based on what I learned. I look forward to that discussion.

Thanks again for your support.

Sincerely,

_____

Do the Preparatory Work Well

To get your money's worth, you need to do more than just do the preparatory work. You need to do it with a will. If the preparation involves reading, read with intensity. Think about what questions you want answers for. Write notes in the margin. Argue with the author. If something strikes you, underline it and make a note. Think of examples from your own experience that support or contradict what is being said.

The more actively you read, the more you elaborate on the text, the better the information sticks (See "Who Says So?"). The better it sticks, the better you will be able to use it to improve your performance.

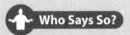 **Who Says So?** *Engagement Matters When Reading*

Multiple studies have shown that active engagement while reading—"elaborative processing" in the psychological jargon—improves retention. For example, students given questions to answer in advance are much better able to recall information than students who studied the same material without advance questions.

Based on an extensive review of the learning literature, Anderson (2005, p. 195) recommends the following PQ4R approach to reading:

1. **Preview**: Survey the material to ascertain the topics being discussed.
2. **Questions**: Think up questions about each of the sections. Often simply turning section headings into questions is sufficient.
3. **Read**: Read each section, trying to answer the questions you have generated.
4. **Reflect**: Reflect on the text as you read. Try to understand it, to come up with examples from your own experience, and to relate what you are reading to what you already know.
5. **Recite**: When you finish a section, try to recall what you have read. See whether you can answer your own questions. If not, reread the section (repetition has a powerful positive effect on recall).
6. **Review**: After you have finished a chapter, review it mentally, trying to recall its key points.

Complete the rest of the preparatory assignments with the same kind of rigor and energy; you will get more out of the whole learning experience if you do.

Plan Your Work, Work Your Plan

Make a plan; schedule the time and set reminders to do the preparation.

1. List the assignments on the checklist provided in this book or, if you prefer, use Worksheet 1.5, the Preparation Planner.
2. Schedule time on your calendar to complete the assignments.
3. Complete the tasks as they come up.
4. Treat them as you would other key business objectives; accept no excuses for late or shoddy work.

WORKSHEET 1.5
Preparation Planner

 **Do It Now**

Instructions: List all the preparatory assignments you have been asked to complete before the training and development program. Check them off as you complete them. In the comments area, jot down your immediate reaction to the value of the assignment and the key "takeaways."

☑	Due Date	Date Finished	Assignment	Comments and Takeaways
☐				
☐				
☐				
☐				
☐				

> **? FAQs** **_What If I Don't Have Time to Do the Preparation?_**
>
> Many years ago—even before the onslaught of electronic communications—Peter Drucker observed that there is no longer enough time to do all the important tasks; you only have time to do what is _very_ important. It may be that your current workload precludes you from doing all the preparation in an optimal fashion.
>
> In that case, you have to prioritize and do the most important. At the top of your list should be self-evaluations, 360-degree feedback instruments, and various pre-tests; these will be key inputs for exercises and action planning.
>
> You may have to just skim the reading, learning to pick out critical issues and insights from the topic headings and lead paragraphs. If you are so overwhelmed with work that you cannot even accomplish these, then consider postponing the training if possible. You may be so ill-prepared and so distracted during the experience that you won't get much value anyway.

2. Get Engaged

The second key to getting your money's worth out of training and development is to get fully engaged in the experience.

Whether you elected to attend the program, or whether you were dragged in kicking and screaming, you'll lose out on much of its potential benefit if you don't actively participate.

The five elements of engagement are:

- ☐ Get your head in the game
- ☐ Get out of your comfort zone
- ☐ Get connected
- ☐ Get specific about what you are going to do
- ☐ Get your story straight

Get Your Head in the Game

To get something out of a learning opportunity, you have to _attend to it_, not merely attend it.

That is, you need to be present mentally as well as physically; you have to give it your full attention (see "Who Says So?"). If you are fiddling with your BlackBerry® or computer, or instant messaging half the time, then your head is never really in the game; your learning (and your subsequent performance) will suffer.

> **Who Says So?** *Learning Needs Your Full Attention*
>
> People greatly overestimate their ability to "multi-task." Indeed, John Medina, director of the Brain Center for Applied Learning Research, declares flatly: "Multi-tasking, when it comes to paying attention, is a myth" (Medina, 2008, p. 84).
>
> The fact is, the human brain has severe "bottlenecks" in its ability to process information (Anderson, 2005, p. 74). We receive so much sensory input all the time that we cannot process it all; we filter out most incoming information. We have to "attend to" specific input for it to rise to a level of consciousness. For example, most of the time we are unaware of the sensory input from our skin—the touch of our clothes or the temperature of our hands—unless we specifically direct our attention to it or it becomes so uncomfortable that it demands our attention. Otherwise we simply ignore it.
>
> When we do direct our attention to one stream of input—when we attend to it—then something else has to be ignored; humans can only pay attention to a very limited number of input channels at once. Think about how you can attend to a specific conversation at a noisy cocktail party and filter out others. To illustrate how powerful this filtering is, Cherry (1953) fitted people with earphones and asked them to listen to two completely different lectures simultaneously—one in each ear. When they were asked to attend to one, for example by repeating it, they often could not remember anything of what was being played into the other ear, even when the message repeated the same phrase multiple times.
>
> An even more dramatic example is the experiment devised by Simons and Chabris (1999). When people were asked to closely attend to a specific action in a video, over 90 percent completely failed to notice a man in a gorilla suit who walked into the center of the action and beat on his chest.
>
> The point is, every time you direct your attention away from the training program to attend to your cell phone, email, etc., you filter out the training and lose some of its potential benefit. Human beings simply cannot attend to multiple input streams simultaneously. Truly "attending" to a conversation is a critical component of active listening and important for business success (Hoppe, 2006). Use the training program as an opportunity to practice "attending."

Similarly, if you rush out at every break and bury yourself in email or voice mail or calls to the office, you lose in two ways:

1. You become distracted and miss the beginning of the next section, either because you are physically late or because you are still mentally focused on other issues.

2. You interact less with other participants and lose the opportunity for networking and learning from others—which may be as important as the course material itself.

> *You need to* attend to *training, not just attend it.*

Seize the opportunity to learn as much as you can while you have the chance. Declare the time you will be in training as an "emergencies only" contact period. Curb your own addiction to being constantly in touch. Let the voicemails and emails sit until the end of the day or even until the end of the program. Treat the time away from the daily grind as a blessing rather than an imposition.

"Dave, could you hold on a sec while I take care of some personal business?"

Look at it this way: If your organization can't run for a few days or even a few hours without you, that raises questions about your ability to organize, delegate, and build a competent team.

THINK

Use the training program as an excuse to stop, catch your breath, and THINK, instead of just react. Expect your team and associates to handle things in your absence; it will be a growth opportunity for them. And if you are an individual contributor with no one to delegate to—take the time anyway. The work will be there when you get back and you will be able to tackle it with fresh perspective, energy, and new skills.

Getting your head in the game is a conscious decision.

- Actively decide you are going to make the most of the opportunity, regardless of what brought you there.

- Suspend disbelief temporarily; open your mind to new ideas and approaches.

- Drop your know-it-all attitude; listen to what others have to say.

- Turn off your cell phone, pager, instant messenger, PDA, etc.

- Practice attending—giving the matter in front of you your undivided attention. It will make you more effective as a learner, as a manager, and as a life partner.

🧠 Think About It   *The Importance of "Attending"*

Has your spouse or significant other ever complained that you were not listening to what he or she was saying? Have you ever been frustrated trying to have a serious conversation with someone who keeps being interrupted, or who is simultaneously answering email or dividing his or her attention between you and the television? Have you ever let your mind wander in a meeting or program and been unable to recall what had just been said?

What these experiences prove is that people cannot truly attend to two things simultaneously. You can switch back and forth, but you cannot attend to both simultaneously. Each switch takes time and loses information (Medina, 2008, p. 87).

Now, think about how you feel when someone does—or does not—attend to what you are saying. For most people, nothing is more irritating than to feel you are being ignored. You will be more effective as a leader, friend, and partner if you develop your ability to truly attend to others.

Get Out of Your Comfort Zone

More careers derail because of poor interpersonal skills than for any other reason (VanVelsor & Leslie, 1995). Use the training program as an opportunity to improve your repertoire of interpersonal skills, even when that is not one of the program's stated objectives.

"Damn It, man, I expect my executives to be more open to new ideas than this."

To do so requires getting out of your comfort zone and consciously changing some habitual behaviors. If you are an extravert, shut up. If you are an introvert, speak up. Participate in role-playing exercises, even if you feel self-conscious; volunteer answers, even though they might be wrong. Play games to win. Take risks in simulations. Experiment with different ways of interacting with other participants and see what happens. You won't find a better opportunity at work.

Admittedly, we all like to look good. We like to give the right answers and appear expert, especially when co-workers, direct reports, or managers are around. We hate to be wrong or look foolish; many of us still carry emotional scars from something we once said or did wrong in school.

Get over it.

You won't get full value out of a training program if you hang back and always let others answer the questions, do the assignments, or lead the group. A training and development program is a great time to experiment with different styles of interaction. Training is the one place in business where there is no serious penalty for screwing up. People learn fastest from their mistakes. Go ahead and make some; you will learn valuable lessons in the process.

Use the Personal Challenge Worksheet (1.6) to set a personal challenge for yourself; use the training to try something outside your natural comfort zone. And, if you find that a different style of interaction yields better results than what you instinctively do, add it to your repertoire.

Get Connected

Learning events are opportunities to expand two networks critical to your success:

- People

- Knowledge

Connect with People

The opportunity to connect with colleagues from different departments, locations, divisions, or companies is a huge benefit of in-person training. Seize it.

Make a conscious effort to sit with people you do not already know. Introduce yourself. Ask about what they do, where they come from, what challenges their businesses face.

Expanding your personal network may be as valuable as the program itself. A large and diverse interpersonal network contributes to business success. (See "Who Says So?")

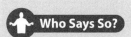 **Who Says So?** *Importance of Networks*

It is advantageous to have a robust interpersonal network.

Who you know and who knows you are paramount to success in your career. People with well-developed networks have access to people, information, and resources to help solve problems and create opportunities (Dulworth, 2008).

An article in MIT's *Sloan Management Review* concluded that "What really distinguishes high performers from the rest of the pack is their ability to maintain and leverage personal networks. The most effective knowledge workers create and tap large, diversified networks that are rich in experience and span all organizational boundaries" (Cross, Davenport, & Cantrell, 2003).

According to the New York firm BH Careers International, only 20 percent of available jobs make it to job boards or the classifieds. Finding a new position, therefore, is far more likely to be accomplished through word-of-mouth than through formal channels.

But networking is not just about finding job opportunities; networks are important sources of new business ideas, critical information, and opportunities to collaborate. You often need information from other departments. If you have a relationship with employees in those departments, they'll be more likely to help you. Social networks are important to the creation and diffusion of innovations. Transformational ideas (like the quartz watch) usually come from people outside the prevailing paradigm. So it is important that your network include people from different fields, companies, and world views.

Finally, social networks contribute to personal health and well-being. Social network size is consistently related to health and well-being and the effects may be as important as weight control, blood pressure, smoking, and physical activity (House, Landis, & Umberson, 1988).

WORKSHEET 1.6
Personal Challenge

Do It Now

Instructions: Read the description below. Choose a few new ways of interacting that you are going to experiment with during the training. Afterward, record your observations (results/reactions) and your intent (do more, do less) going forward.

Category	My Usual Response	I Am Going to Try	Result/Reaction	Plan Going Forward:
Questions/Team Reports	☐ Jump in with the answers	☐ Consciously wait to encourage others to participate		☐ Do more ☐ Do less ☐ Other: _____
	☐ Hang back and let others answer	☐ Force myself to volunteer answers more often		☐ Do more ☐ Do less ☐ Other: _____
Role Play and Demonstrations	☐ Volunteer immediately; enjoy being in front of the group.	☐ Hang back, encourage others to have a turn		☐ Do more ☐ Do less ☐ Other: _____
	☐ Try my best not to be picked to demonstrate	☐ Force myself to volunteer to be one of the players		☐ Do more ☐ Do less ☐ Other: _____
Teamwork and Group Exercises	☐ Step into the leadership role. Take charge; organize the work.	☐ Consciously encourage others to lead the group; practice followership		☐ Do more ☐ Do less ☐ Other: _____
	☐ Be a great team player and support whoever takes the lead, but don't lead myself	☐ Step up to the leadership role; ask to lead if some- one else is always taking charge		☐ Do more ☐ Do less ☐ Other: _____

If you make the effort to connect with others in the program, you may find opportunities to serve common customers, complementary offerings, process improvements, or even a whole new business idea that you otherwise would never have discovered. When you interact with people from different disciplines and organizations, you are bound to learn something. Open yourself to the possibilities.

 **Think About It**   *Value of Relationships*

Who would you be more willing to help or share information with: a complete stranger or someone you met at a training program, worked with on some of the exercises, and with whom you had an engaging discussion over lunch?

To help you make the most of the interpersonal connection opportunities, complete the Human Connections form (Worksheet 1.7) for at least three new people at the program.

Connect the Dots

It is one thing to learn something new; it is another to *remember* what you have learned so that you are able to recall it later when you need it. Most people are much better at learning than remembering.

Here are four things you can do to increase your ability to recall what you learn:

"What does he know, and how long will he know it?"

- Find the connections
- Draw the links
- Space learning over time
- Write it down

Find the Connections

Finding connections means actively looking for links between the new material and what you already know and have experienced.

WORKSHEET 1.7
Interpersonal Connections

Do It Now

Instructions

1. Try to meet at least three new people at the learning event (or people you know only by name or reputation). Spend enough time with them at breaks, meals, and so forth so that you can complete the connections table below.

2. In addition to each person's name, find out what his or her job is—not just the title, but what it entails. Help yourself connect with this person by linking his or her name to something interesting and personal— a hobby, a place the person has lived or traveled, an interesting experience he or she has had, etc.

3. Listen for something that you have in common—a common work experience, a favorite kind of food, place to visit, family background, anything that helps you connect.

4. Finally, think about a possible business connection—could he or she be a consultant, a potential employee, a resource, a collaborator, or play some other role? The point is not whether you ultimately pursue any one of these ideas, but to train yourself to always be on the lookout for such opportunities.

Complete the chart below for at least three new people:

Person's Name	What does he/she do for a living?	Something interesting about him/her personally	Something the two of you have in common	Potential business connection with this person

As you listen, read, discuss, or practice, think of examples. Try to come up with other things you've learned or experienced that reinforce (or even contradict) what is being taught. Key phrases include: "This is just like . . ." "That reminds me of . . ." "I know exactly what you mean because I once . . . " "That doesn't match with my experience. . . ."

Why is this important? Because the more connections something has—the more "hooks" to your knowledge and experience—the easier it is to recall later.

Draw the Links

You may want to try taking notes as an "idea map" instead of just bullets or lists. Use color, pictures, lines, arrows—whatever will help you visualize the connections among ideas. Many people have an easier time recalling information from an idea map than from traditional notes or texts (Buzan, 1996). An example is shown in Figure 1.2.

Figure 1.2

An Example of a Mind Map to Help Remember the Six Disciplines of Breakthrough Learning

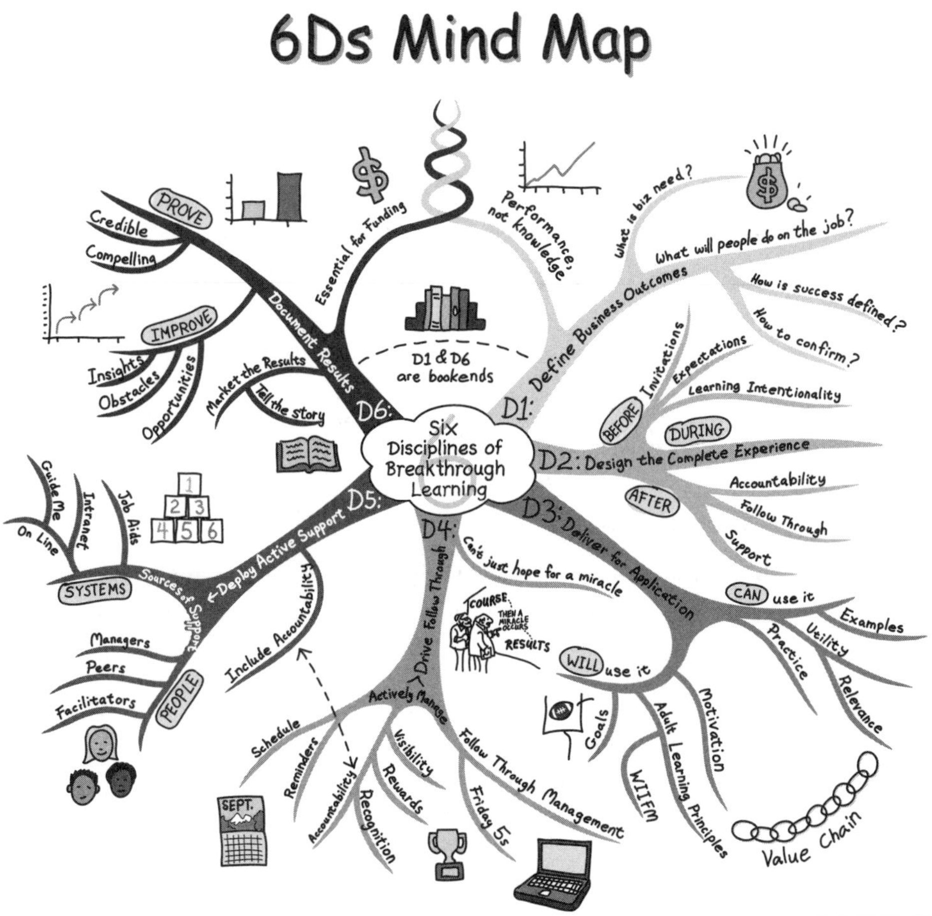

Who Says So? *Spacing Improves Recall*

The effects of practice on memory are well known and highly predictable. Each time we use a memory trace, we increase its strength and improve the efficiency of recall. This relationship between practice and recall is known as the Power Law of Learning; the time to retrieve an item from memory decreases as a logarithmic function of the amount of practice (Anderson, 2005, p. 188).

In addition, practice increases retention. The Power Law of Forgetting describes the relationship between practice and remembering. The more practice and the shorter the interval between practice and use, the more can be recalled (Wixted & Ebbesen, 1991). "Indeed, repeated exposure to information in specifically timed intervals provides the most powerful way to fix memory into the brain" (Medina, 2008, p. 132).

Thalheimer (2006) reviewed the research on spaced learning and concluded:

1. Repetitions—if well designed—are very effective.

2. Spacing is particularly beneficial if long-term retention is the goal.

3. Spacing helps minimize forgetting.

4. Wider spacing is generally more effective than narrower spacing.

5. One-time events rarely produce real learning.

Space Learning Over Time

Finally, spacing your learning over time will help you master any subject. The value of spacing is one of the most well-studied effects in learning. (See "Who Says So?")

If you can return to the topic, idea map, reading, etc., several times over days or weeks, you will develop much deeper and more durable learning than when you try to cram everything into one session. If the program lasts several days, take advantage of the spacing effect by reviewing your prior notes and idea maps before beginning each subsequent session. Look for opportunities to incorporate ideas from the beginning of the program into your thinking and notes as the program progresses.

Write It Down

Finally, take the time to summarize your thoughts on paper. Write them down. The act of summarizing and writing out what you learned will help you remember and retain it.

A good habit is to pause at the end of each section of the program before you go on break; stop, think, and write down the answer to the following question: "If the program were to end right now, what could I use and what would the benefit be?" Use the WIIFM Recap form (Worksheet 1.8) to help you.

WORKSHEET 1.8
Recap WIIFM

Instructions: At the end of each topic or segment of the course, take a few minutes to complete the table below.

Topic or Segment	Big "Aha" or Idea I Could Use	Benefit/Payoff

? **FAQs**   *What If the Training Is Not Working for Me?*

When you participate in a learning program, you invest your time. And, given the pace of business these days, your time is precious. Therefore, you have a right to expect something of value in return. Be a respectful, but demanding, customer.

If you have done your homework, if you have thought about what you want to get out of the experience, and if you are fully engaged, but the program is still not delivering value for you, then you should do something about it.

Start by speaking up. If you do not understand the connection between the course and the needs of the business, ask for clarification. Check with your classmates. If you are the only one who is having trouble seeing the on-the-job relevance, don't dominate the airwaves; ask the instructor during a break or after class or ask your peers to explain it. But if others are also struggling to see the point as well, then everyone will benefit if you ask the instructor to relate topics or exercises to the larger business context.

Alternatively, the content may be relevant, but you already know everything that is being presented. Of course, it is unlikely that you know everything; you can probably still learn something new or from a different perspective. But it could be that you really do know the material as well as or nearly as well as the instructor so that the benefit for you is low in relation to the time you are having to invest.

In that case, you have a few choices. If it is a voluntary program, you can politely excuse yourself at the next break explaining that you signed up for the wrong program. If attendance is mandatory, then use the opportunity to add value to the company by teaching others what you know; you will reinforce your own knowledge in the process.

Finally, even in a well-managed company, there is an occasional program that is poorly designed, badly taught, or that otherwise misses the mark. Regardless of your position in the company, you have a responsibility to do something about it; don't just walk way and forget it. Doing so causes your colleagues to also waste their time.

Rock the boat. Make your concerns clear on the end-of-course evaluation; don't take the easy route and just check middle-of-the-road scores. Express your concerns to your manager and the head of training. Provide constructive criticism and suggestions for making the program more useful, relevant, and applicable. You are a customer, after all. You paid for the program with your time. You have a right to be heard.

Get Specific About What You Are Going to Do

The value of any learning experience depends entirely on what you *do* with it. Learning that isn't put to use is scrap—a waste of everyone's time and money.

To get your money's worth from training and development, you need to set clear goals and formulate an action plan for putting your learning to work. That is why goal-setting and action-planning exercises are included in so many programs. But even if goal setting is not part of the formal program, you will benefit by establishing strong and stretch objectives for yourself. (See Who Says So?)

> ### 👤 Who Says So? *You Should Set Personal Goals*
>
> Setting a small number of personally-meaningful goals is important to success across a wide range of occupations and endeavors.
>
> A characteristic of outstanding sales people, for example, is that they have specific and challenging business targets that they set for themselves. These are coupled to very clear personal ambitions for what they want to achieve with the rewards of business success (Cameron & Green, 2004). Top performers in every field studied—from business, to chess, from sports to performing arts—consistently set stretch goals for themselves; exceptional performers never cease trying to further improve (Ericsson, Prietula, & Cokely, 2007).
>
> Specific, written goals are important. If you want to get things done, according to productivity expert, David Allen (2001), you need to get them into a system, "outside of your head and off your mind." Writing down what you want to accomplish is an important first step. David Campbell of the Center for Creative Leadership put it this way: "If you do not know where you are going, you will probably end up someplace else" (Campbell, 1974).
>
> Your goals should be personally meaningful, but not private. Share them with others, because you will be more likely to achieve them if you do. "Social psychologists learned long ago that if you make a commitment and then share it with friends, you're far more likely to follow-through than if you simply make your commitment to yourself" (Patterson, Grenny, Maxfield, McMillan, & Switzler 2008, p. 152).

Select just one to three things you want to accomplish using your newly acquired knowledge and skills and enter them into a learning contract with your manager. Build on your strengths and, whenever possible, link your new objectives to work goals you already have so that you are using your existing priorities as your "practice field" rather that creating a whole new "to do."

If your course does not supply a goal form, use Worksheet 1.9. Evaluate your objective using the checklist.

Once you have defined your goals for applying what you learned and have thought through the challenges and the help you need, you are almost ready for the third and final step in getting your money's worth: getting results. But before you head back to work . . . get your story straight.

Get Your Story Straight

When you return to work, you will have a golden opportunity to demonstrate that you used your time well and that you can continue to learn and grow. That's essential if you want to earn greater responsibility and respect. To take advantage of this opportunity, you need a well-thought-out "elevator speech."

The idea of the elevator speech originated at Xerox. The premise is that if a senior manager steps on to the elevator and says to you, "So, tell

WORKSHEET 1.9
Goals for Applying Learning

Do It Now

Instructions: If your program does not include a goal-setting exercise, complete the worksheet below. Select one to no more than three things you want to accomplish using the new knowledge and skills acquired in the program. Think through the first steps you need to take, potential barriers to progress, and what will help you achieve your objectives.

GOAL 1

In the next _____ (weeks/months), _____ [specify what you will accomplish].

The benefit to me and the organization will be: _____ [explain the value].

Evidence of progress and success will include _____

_____ [define the indicators of progress and measures of success].

My first action(s) upon returning to work will be:

1. _____
2. _____
3. _____

Potential impediments to progress and my plans to minimize them include:

Potential Impediment	Plan to Mitigate or Remove

Given the above, the most important help I will need to achieve these goals is:

Help Needed	From Whom

GOAL 2

In the next _____ (weeks/months), _____ [specify what you will accomplish].

The benefit to me and the organization will be: _____ [explain the value].

Evidence of progress and success will include _____

_____ [define the indicators of progress and measures of success].

My first action(s) upon returning to work will be:

1. _____
2. _____
3. _____

Potential impediments to progress and my plans to minimize them include:

Potential Impediment	Plan to Mitigate or Remove

Given the above, the most important help I will need to achieve these goals is:

Help Needed	From Whom

Test your goal against the following benchmarks:

☐ I have defined just one, two, or three key things to accomplish.

☐ They require that I use and practice newly acquired skills and knowledge.

☐ They are connected to my existing priorities; I am using work I have to do anyway as my "practice field."

☐ They are specific about what I will accomplish and when.

☐ They require some "stretch" but are achievable in the time allotted.

"What does it look like, Sam? I'm running a little late this morning."

me about your idea," you will have roughly thirty seconds between the lobby and the fourth floor to explain it. If you can quickly and clearly articulate your main points, you will advance your idea and career. Conversely, if you are unable to explain the essence before the doors opened again, the opportunity is lost forever—a career-limiting move.

In the case of training, your manager and associates are almost certain to ask you about your experience when you return to work. To seize this opportunity, you need a clear, succinct statement about what you learned, how you plan to use it, and how it will help you and your group. If you don't have one, you'll blow an exceptional opportunity.

Use Worksheet 1.10 to get your story straight before you head back to the office. What are the key points you want to communicate about the training, your objectives, the value you will generate, and any help you might need? Now is the time to ask.

3. Get Results

The real work begins when the training ends. All your preparation, all your participation, all the best teaching in the world won't do a bit of good unless you apply it.

For many years, organizations treated the last day of class as if it were the "finish line" for training and development. Certificates were awarded for completing the course . . . and not much happened afterward.

Nowadays, pressure for performance and return on investment demands a new finish line: on-the-job results. You're not done until you have *transferred* what you learned to your job and have used it in ways that improve your own and the business's performance. To meet expectations, you need to get results.

The keys to getting results after training are to:

☐ Get reconnected

☐ Get going (and keep at it)

☐ Get the help you need

☐ Get better

☐ Get ready to do it again

WORKSHEET 1.10
Elevator Speech

Do It Now

Instructions: Complete the four sentences below. If time permits, practice your elevator speech with a partner.

1. The most important/striking/insightful/valuable (pick one) thing I learned was: _____
   _____

2. I am going to capitalize on this learning by: _____
   _____

3. The benefit for our organization will be: _____
   _____

4. I'll need the following help to make this happen: _____
   _____

Get Reconnected

When you return to work—even if your absence has been brief—your first task is to reconnect with your colleagues and manager.

The first day is critical. That's when people will be interested in your experience and will ask you about it. It's a great opportunity to make the points in your elevator speech. Wander around intentionally to give people a chance to ask you. Don't wait; the opportunity is short-lived. If you delay only a day or two, people will have forgotten that you were gone and you will have missed your chance.

Share What You Learned

Relating your experience to others also helps you; there is no better way to learn something than to teach it to someone else. As you talk to your colleagues about what you learned, try to explain a key concept or insight you had. You will benefit as much as they do. Better yet, write a short memo to your colleagues summarizing the most valuable points and how they apply to the work of your unit. Or offer to make a short presentation or give a demonstration at a staff meeting or a "brown-bag" lunch. You'll benefit in several ways:

- The preparation and delivery will reinforce and deepen your own understanding and skill.
- You'll help your colleagues improve, which benefits everyone.
- You'll get a valuable reputation as a leader, learner, and collaborator.

Say "Thank You"

If the program involved feedback from your peers, direct reports, or manager, make it a point to follow up and thank everyone who contributed. It is very important that you do (see Who Says So?).

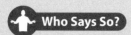 **Who Says So?**   *You Should Follow Up with Feedback Providers*

When people invest their time and effort to provide you with feedback, they want to know that their efforts were appreciated and that their message was received. Their hopes have been raised that you will work on areas of potential improvement. At a minimum, they would like to know what you intend to do with the input. Your follow-up—or lack of it—shapes their opinion of your potential.

Goldsmith and Morgan (2004) analyzed the results of more than eleven thousand managers in eight companies who had received feedback and leadership training. All eight companies tracked the perceived change in leadership effectiveness as judged by co-workers in mini-surveys several months later. They also assessed the extent to which those receiving feedback had follow-up discussions with their co-workers.

They found a strong correlation between follow-up discussions and improved effectiveness. The leaders who were seen as having followed up consistently were far more likely to be rated as "much more effective" than those who did little or no follow-up. Goldsmith put it succinctly: "Leaders who don't follow up, don't improve!."

Bottom line: To be more effective—and to be perceived as more effective—you need to follow up with those who took the time to give you feedback. The best place to start is by saying "thank you," even if some of the feedback was hard to hear.

Your colleagues invested their time and energy providing input; they will be interested in the results. Be prepared to discuss the key themes that emerged in your feedback and, importantly, what you plan to work on. Ask for some feedforward (see FAQ: What Is Feedforward?).

 FAQs   *What Is Feedforward?*

Feedback consists of observations and reactions to past behavior. In contrast, feedforward focuses on the future—what you can do to improve your performance going forward. Since we can change the future, but not the past, feedforward is more action-oriented, less personal, and easier to accept than feedback.

When you return from a development program that includes 360-degree feedback, share with people what you learned and what you plan to focus on. Then ask for some feedforward as follows:

Describe a behavior that you would like to change—something that will make a significant, positive difference in your life and effectiveness.

☐ Ask for feedforward—one or two suggestions for future actions that could help achieve a positive change in this behavior.

☐ Listen attentively to the suggestions and take notes.

☐ Regardless of what you think of the suggestion, do not to comment on it, not even to make positive judgmental statements, such as, "That's a good idea." Just thank the other person for his or her input.

For more information see: www.marshallgoldsmithlibrary.com/cim/articles_display.php?aid=110

You will need other people's help and support to apply what you learned, especially since you won't be proficient in the new approach at first. Going public with your goals—sharing your intent with others both formally and informally—is one of the most important things you can do to help achieve them.

It is especially important that you reconnect with your manager, since he/she has a profound influence on whether or not you achieve your objectives and on your career as a whole.

Ideally, you should have scheduled a follow-up meeting with your manager as part of your pre-course discussion. If you haven't, do it now. Send a meeting request or reminder along the following lines: "I have scheduled a meeting with you on _____ at _____ to go over what I learned in the program I attended recently, how I will use it, the benefits, and the help I need." Use Worksheet 1.11 to help you prepare.

If the program you attended uses an electronic follow-through management system, your manager will automatically receive a copy of your goals. You should still meet with him or her in person or by phone to review your goals, action plan, and the support you need to maximize the value of the investment.

 FAQs   ***What If My Manager Is Too Busy to Meet with Me After the Program?***

If your manager is too busy to meet with you soon after you get back, don't let that stand in the way of your development. Type up a short memo following the guidelines suggested for the post-course meeting (Worksheet 1.11) meeting and send it to him or her. You may or may not receive a response. But at least you will have made the effort and ensured that there should be "no surprises" about what you are working on and why.

If your manager is repeatedly too busy to meet with you about your development, that is abrogation of a key management responsibility. But you must not let it hold back your personal and career development. Find another mentor, someone whose opinion you value and who has a genuine interest in seeing you succeed.

Ultimately, you may want to find another manager who takes a greater interest in your development and makes the time to support you.

Get Going (and Keep at It)

Put your learning to work as soon as you can. Knowledge is most ephemeral when it is brand new. You've got to use it or lose it. (See "Who Says So?"). The longer you delay, the less you can remember and the harder it is to start.

WORKSHEET 1.11
Post-Course Meeting

 **Do It Now**

Instructions: Prepare to meet your manager soon after attending the program by adapting your elevator speech as suggested below.

As you know, I attended the _____ program on _____.

Overall, I found it _____.

The most valuable [thing I learned, insight I gained, exercise we did, etc.] was: _____

_____ which [was /was not] in line

with the focus for my learning we discussed beforehand.

My goals for applying what I learned are:

1. _____.

2. _____.

I expect the benefit for our department to be _____

_____.

The greatest challenges I see in achieving my objectives are _____

_____.

Therefore, I will especially appreciate your help with: _____.

What suggestions do you have regarding my goals or plans?

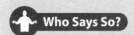 **Who Says So?**   *You Need to Start Using Learning Immediately*

Start using what you learned as soon as possible. New knowledge is lost most rapidly at the beginning. Figure 1.3 illustrates the "power curve of forgetting." As you can see, retention falls rapidly the longer the delay between learning and use. Hence it is very important to start putting what you learned to work as soon as possible. Sharing key insights, methods, and "lessons learned" with others is a good way to reinforce learning and slow the rate of decay (Medina, 2008, p. 131).

Figure 1.3.

Power Curve of Forgetting. The Longer the Delay Between Learning and Use, the More Is Forgotten.

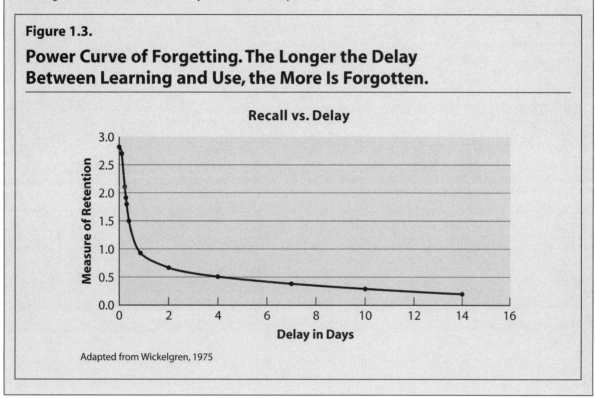

Adapted from Wickelgren, 1975

So, even though you probably accumulated a lot of unanswered emails, messages, and tasks while you were away, start implementing your action plan as soon as possible. Take the first actions you defined as part of your goal-setting process. Record what you did and the results in your online updates. Or, if your program does not yet use a follow-through management system, use Worksheet 1.12.

Keep Going

A good start is important; but it is only that—a start. Real improvement takes sustained effort over time.

WORKSHEET 1.12
First Steps

Do It Now

Instructions: Write down the first three things you need to do to get started on your goals. Do them. Then record the date completed and the results or lessons learned.

✓	Critical First Steps	Date Completed	Results and Learnings
☐			
☐			
☐			

Studies of peak performance in sports, business, the arts, and other fields all point to the same conclusion: what differentiates the great from the not-so-great in any human endeavor is the amount of time they devote to deliberate practice with coaching. (See "Who Says So?")

Who Says So? *Practice Is More Important Than Talent*

When researchers from around the world gathered to discuss "The Acquisition of Expert Performance," they concluded that "natural talent" was overrated. Rather, what characterized experts in fields as diverse as the arts, sciences, sports and games was the amount of deliberate practice in which they had engaged (Ericsson, Prietula, & Cokely, 1995).

Deliberate practice is conscious repetition that focuses on technique as much as results. Deliberate practice includes performance feedback and reflection. What contributed to a positive outcome and should be continued? What detracted from the desired outcome and should be reduced or avoided?

Writing in *Fortune,* Geoffrey Colvin (2006) summarized the findings this way: "The evidence, scientific as well as anecdotal, seems overwhelmingly in favor of deliberate practice as the source of great performance." He goes on to ask, "How do you practice business?" The answer is "all about how you do what you're already doing—you create the practice in your work ... going at any task with a new goal: Instead of merely trying to get it done, you aim to get better at it."

To improve your performance, you need to deliberately practice your new skills and behaviors for weeks and actively seek feedback along the way.

The key is to establish a schedule and stick to it. Put reminders on your scheduling system and enroll others to help remind you of the need to practice. Such cues are important to maintain "share of mind" for your personal development goals.

If your group is using an electronic follow-through management system, you will be reminded automatically every two to four weeks and given a place to record your progress, reflections, and plans. When the reminder arrives, stop, and take the opportunity to reflect, recalibrate, and recharge. Respond to the first request; the longer you put off acting on your objectives, the harder it is to get back to them.

If you do not have such a system available to you, create one by scheduling a reminder in your calendar to stop, reflect, and write down:

- What have I done to make progress toward my goal?

- How much progress did I make?

- What do I need to do next?

If you do not have access to an online system, use the progress chart (Worksheet 1.13) to track your progress. Post it above your desk so you do not forget to reflect on your progress periodically.

WORKSHEET 1.13
Plot Your Progress

Do It Now

Instructions: Every two weeks, plot your progress toward achieving your learning application goals using the chart below. Post the chart prominently in your work space.

Objective achieved

Significant Progress

Moderate Progress

Slight Progress

None yet

Notes:

Week: 0   2   4   6   8   10

———————— Goal 1   ------------------ Goal 2

When it comes to development, "slow and steady wins the race." It is more important to have the discipline to maintain your effort over time than to start with a burst of energy but then run out of steam before you have established new and more effective habits.

Get the Help You Need

No athlete ever made it to the Olympics without a coach. No musician ever played at Carnegie Hall without having studied under a master. People at the top of their game in business always credit mentors they have had along the way (see "Who Says So?"). Don't try to do it all yourself; reach out to those who can help you make faster, better progress, and ask for their help.

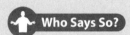 **Who Says So?**   *Mentors and Coaches Matter*

People who have worked with mentors have more promotions, greater incomes, increased career satisfaction and increased job mobility compared to those without mentors (Schweibert, 2000).

The importance of mentors transcends occupations. For example, professors who had mentors within their organizations had the highest levels of objective career success (Peluchette & Jeanquart, 2000). Managers who had mentors had higher "promotability" ratings than managers who did not participate in a mentoring program (Shelton, 1982). Both mentors and their protégés in nursing experienced greater career success and satisfaction (Vance & Olsen, 1998).

Trusted advisors provide both career and psychosocial support. They can play a critical role in showing you "the ropes" in a career transition, in helping you gain perspective on challenges and on your strengths and weaknesses. Mentors can also provide much needed support and sympathetic listening in times of crisis. Virtually no one reaches peak performance without the help of a coach and mentor.

To get your money's worth from training and development, find and use a trusted coach or mentor.

"I'd like you to excel."

Although it may sound like an oxymoron, personal development is actually a team sport. You need the perspective and advice of others to be the best you can be. Check in with other participants in the class, your manager, or another trusted advisor. Seek input on your progress and how you can further improve your execution. It's what every great performer in every field does.

Other sources of support include books and articles, course materials, online references, instructors, fellow learners, and professional coaches. If your program uses a follow-through support system, some of these will be built in. You may also be provided with recommended readings, access to subject-matter experts, and other support systems and materials. Use Worksheet 1.14 to help you think about the kinds of support that will help you the most.

If you list people as sources of support, you'll need to get their agreement to play that role. Remember that when someone agrees to act as your coach or mentor, that person is committing his or her time and taking a chance on you. You will need to hold up your end of the bargain by genuinely considering your advisor's advice and making a sincere, ongoing effort to improve.

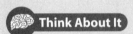 **Think About It** *What Would You Expect?*

Suppose someone approached you and asked you to be his or her mentor. You would be flattered, of course. But beyond that, what would you expect of the person you have agreed to help?

If you invested your time, energy, and reputation to provide advice and he or she did nothing, how would you feel?

Now think about how those answers apply to you when you are the one being mentored.

Get Better

The real finish line for learning is not the last day of class, but when you can demonstrate improved performance at work as a result of using what you have learned. Continue your efforts—practicing, reflecting, seeking feedback—until you have reached a new and higher level of performance, until the progress you have made is evident to those around you.

It will take weeks to months to prove that the change is sustainable. Remember that people's perception will lag behind the actual changes you have made. You have to keep at it. Your learning is complete only when you are "consciously competent" at a new (and higher) level of performance.

"George Tully is a really first-rate individual, up from second-rate this past quarter."

Close the Loop

Finally, close the loop. When you have achieved a new level of skill and competence, schedule

WORKSHEET 1.14
Sources of Support

Do It Now

Instructions: Check the sources of support that you think will be of most interest/value to you personally, given your goals and job responsibilities.

Plan to Use	Source	What I hope to get from this source:
☐	My manager	
☐	A fellow participant Who? _____	
☐	Another colleague Who? _____	
☐	Reading Title:_____	
☐	Online materials Which? _____	
☐	Course materials Specifically:_____	
☐	A subject-matter expert Who? _____	
☐	A course instructor Who? _____	
☐	My direct reports	

a meeting to share the results with your manager. Show how investing in you has paid off, and be prepared to discuss the next phase of your developmental journey—in other words, get ready to do it all again.

Get Ready to Do It Again

Congratulations. When you have practiced applying your new skills and knowledge to the point that they are now your new norm—when you do them routinely and well—you have completed this round of development. But you cannot rest on your laurels. The world moves on. Demands and expectations increase; your competitors improve their game. You need to continue to learn, grow, and adapt.

> *The ability to learn faster than your competitors may be the only sustainable competitive advantage.*
> —Arie deGues

Which brings you back to the beginning of a new cycle. Complete Worksheet 1.15, schedule a meeting, and discuss it with your manager. What were your most important learnings and achievements in this cycle? How can you improve your performance even further? That might include taking another course, reading or self-study, a stretch assignment, mentoring from an expert, etc.

Many different routes can take you to your destination, as long as you are clear about where you want to go. Get your manager's input. If you demonstrate the initiative, your organization will provide opportunities and resources.

> *All development is self-development.*
> —Peter Drucker

Enjoy the Ride

Good luck and safe travels on the quest to be all you can be. It is an exciting and rewarding journey. Enjoy the trip and send us a postcard. We'd like to hear how you are doing and how we can make this guide even better for those who come after you.

WORKSHEET 1.15
Close the Loop

 **Do It Now**

Instructions: Use this worksheet to help you plan a final meeting with your manager to "close the loop" on this round of development and to plan for the future.

Program you attended: _____

Date: _____

What you consider your most important achievement or improvement that resulted from your attendance and follow-through:

_____

_____

_____

Specific examples/evidence:

_____

_____

_____

What do you think you should work on next? [List three things that—if you could do them even faster, better, and more effectively—would make you even more valuable than you are today. In some cases, the most important thing will be to sustain, extend, or deepen the capabilities and skills you developed in this round.]

  1. _____

  2. _____

  3. _____

Seek your manager's agreement with your achievements and plan for future development. Ask for her/his ideas on the best opportunities to continue to learn and improve your performance.

References and Additional Reading for Participants

Allen, D. (2001). *Getting things done.* New York: Penguin.

Anderson, J.R. (2005). *Cognitive psychology and its implications.* New York: Freeman.

Brinkerhoff, R.O., & Apking, A.M. (2001). *High impact learning: Strategies for leveraging business results from training.* New York: Basic Books.

Brinkerhoff, R.O., & Montesino, M. (1995). Partnerships for learning transfer: Lessons from a corporate study. *Human Resource Development Quarterly, 6*(3), 263–274.

Broad, M.L., & Newstrom, J.W. (1992). *Transfer of training: Action-packed strategies to ensure high payoff from training investments.* Cambridge, MA: Perseus.

Buzan, T. (1996). *The mind map book.* New York: Penguin.

Cameron, E., & Green, M. (2004). *Making sense of change management: A complete guide to the models, tools and techniques of organizational change.* London: Kogan Page.

Campbell, D. (1974). *If you don't know where you're going, you'll probably end up somewhere else.* Valencia, CA: Tabor.

Cherry, E.C. (1953). Some experiments on the recognition of speech, with one and with two ears. *Journal of the Acoustical Society of America, 23,* 915–919.

Colvin, G: (2006, October). What it takes to be great. *Fortune,* pp. 88–96.

Cross, R., Davenport, T., & Cantrell, S. (2003). The social side of high performance. *Sloan Management Review, 45*(1) pp. 20–24.

Dempster, F.N. (1989). Spacing effects and their implications for theory and practice. *Educational Psychology Review, 1,* 309–330.

Dulworth, M. (2008) *The connect effect: Building strong personal, professional, and virtual networks.* San Francisco: Berrett-Kohler.

Ericsson, K.A., Prietula, M.J., & Cokely, E. (2007, August). The making of an expert. *Harvard Business Review,* pp. 115–121.

Goldsmith, M. & Morgan, H. (2004). Leadership is a contact sport: The follow-up factor in leadership development. *Strategy + Business, 37*, 71–79.

Hoppe, M.H. (2006). *Active listening: Improve your ability to listen and lead.* Greensboro, NC: Center for Creative Leadership.

House, J.S., Landis, K.R., & Umberson, D. (1988). Social relationships and health. *Science, 241*, 540–545.

Medina, J. (2008). *Brain rules: 12 principles for surviving and thriving at work, home and school.* Seattle, WA: Pear Press.

Patterson, K., Grenny, J., Maxfield, D., McMillan, R., & Switzler, A. (2008). *Influencer: The power to change anything.* New York: McGraw-Hill.

Peluchette, J.V., & Jeanquart, S. (2000). Professionals' use of different mentor sources at various career stages: Implications for career success. *Journal of Social Psychology, 140*(5), 549–564.

Schweibert, V. (2000). *Mentoring: Creating connected, empowered relationships.* Alexandria, VA: American Counseling Association.

Shelton, C.K. (1990). The relationship of mentoring and behavioral style to selected job success variables. Thesis (Ed. D.). DeKalb, IL: Northern Illinois University, 1982.

Simons, D.J., & Chabris, C.E. (1999). Gorillas in our midst: Sustained inattention blindness for dynamic events. *Perception, 28*, 1059–1074.

Thalheimer, W. (2006). *Spacing learning events over time: What the research says.* Retrieved May 26, 2008, from www.work-learning.com/catalog/

Vance, C., & Olsen, R. (1998). *The mentor connection in nursing.* New York: Springer.

VanVelsor, E., & Leslie, J.B. (1995). Why executives derail: Perspectives across time and cultures. *Academy of Management Executive, 9*, 62–72.

Wixted, J.T., & Ebbesen, E. (1991). On the form of forgetting. *Psychological Science, 2*, 409–415.

Wick, C., Pollock, R., Jefferson, A., & Flanagan, R. (2006). *The six disciplines of breakthrough learning: How to turn training and development into business results.* San Francisco: Pfeiffer.

Wickelgren, W. (1975). Alcohol intoxication and memory storage dynamics. *Memory and Cognition, 3*, 385–389.

Appendix

Completed Examples for Participants*

COMPLETED EXAMPLE OF WORKSHEET 1.1
Opportunities for Improvement

 **Do It Now**

Instructions: List three things that, if you could do them faster, better, or more effectively, would make you even more valuable than you are today:

1. Be better about catching people "doing something right" and saying something positive about it on the spot.

2. Giving feedback to my peers when I feel they are not being team players or working in the best interest of the company as a whole.

3. Delegate more; stop getting bogged down in tasks that others can do. Stop being so shy about asking people to do their jobs.

---

*Additional examples are available on the book's website, www.pfeiffer.com/go/forthill
Once on the website, use the password **reference** to access the files.

COMPLETED EXAMPLES OF WORKSHEET 1.2
WIIFM for Participants

Example 1

Your Name: _Pat O'Brian_

Name of Program: _High-Impact Marketing_   Date of Program: _11/12/08_

	Most important deliverables of my business/ organizational unit	Most important results for which I am personally responsible	What new or improved skills/ knowledge would help me deliver better results	Topics covered in the training or development program	Therefore, what I want to get out of it (be able to do better or differently)
Your Input	revenue growth sustained profitability	effective marketing programs strong branding perceived value	better segmenting and targeting more effective project mgt	positioning segmentation/ targeting product life cycle management selecting vendors	improve the way I segment and target campaigns to increase impact
Your Manager's Review	☐ Agree as written ☐ See edits ☐ Let's discuss	☐ Agree as written ☐ See edits ☐ Let's discuss	☐ Agree as written ☐ See edits ☐ Let's discuss	☐ Agree as written ☐ See edits ☐ Let's discuss	☐ Agree as written ☐ See edits ☐ Let's discuss
Comments:					

Example 2

Your Name: _Jane Jonson_

Name of Program: _Delivering Customer Delight_   Date of Program: _2/12/09_

	Most important deliverables of my business/ organizational unit	Most important results for which I am personally responsible	What new or improved skills/ knowledge would help me deliver better results	Topics covered in the training or development program	Therefore, what I want to get out of it (be able to do better or differently)
Your Input	customer satisfaction	timely and accurate response to inquiries rapid and fair resolution of complaints/claims	better conflict-resolution skills better ability to empathize on phone	the customer service challenge getting to yes active listening handling difficult customers	improve my ability to more quickly reach resolution that the customer feels is fair
Your Manager's Review	☐ Agree as written ☐ See edits ☐ Let's discuss	☐ Agree as written ☐ See edits ☐ Let's discuss	☐ Agree as written ☐ See edits ☐ Let's discuss	☐ Agree as written ☐ See edits ☐ Let's discuss	☐ Agree as written ☐ See edits ☐ Let's discuss
Comments:					

COMPLETED EXAMPLES OF WORKSHEET 1.3
Learning Contract

Example 1

YOUR COMMITMENT

In order to maximize the value of my learning and development in the upcoming <u>Parts Department Management</u> program, I agree to:

- ☑ Complete all required pre-course reading and other assignments
- ☑ Attend and be actively engaged in all sessions
- ☑ Develop goals for applying what I learned to my work
- ☑ Execute a follow-through plan that improves my performance
- ☑ Report the results
- ☑ Share highlights and insights with my co-workers
- ☑ <u>Seek out and bring back Best Practices from other dealerships</u>

Specifically, I will focus on <u>inventory management</u> during the program in order to improve <u>my ability to maximize profitability and efficiency of repair process</u> afterward.

Signed: <u>Malcolm Rogers</u>

Date: <u>July 23, 2009</u>

Example 2

YOUR COMMITMENT

In order to maximize the value of my learning and development in the upcoming <u>New Manager Orientation</u> program, I agree to:

- ☑ Complete all required pre-course reading and other assignments
- ☑ Attend and be actively engaged in all sessions
- ☑ Develop goals for applying what I learned to my work
- ☑ Execute a follow-through plan that improves my performance
- ☑ Report the results
- ☑ Share highlights and insights with my co-workers

Specifically, I will focus on <u>performance management and giving effective feedback</u> during the program in order to improve <u>my team's performance and individuals' clear sense of direction and being valued</u> afterward.

Signed: <u>Suzanna Wu</u>

Date: <u>August 3, 2009</u>

COMPLETED EXAMPLE OF WORKSHEET 1.4
Learning Memorandum

Do It Now

Dear <u>Margaret,</u>

Thank you for meeting with me today to discuss the upcoming <u>Leader to Leader</u> Program.

We agreed that the most important thing for me to focus on during the course was <u>improving my ability to communicate a compelling vision that others want to contribute to and make happen</u> in order to improve my performance in the area of <u>leadership and team building</u>

You agreed to make sure that I had the time to do the assignments, attend the program with minimum interruptions, and have opportunities to practice my new skills / knowledge afterward. You also agreed to provide coaching so that I can benefit from your expertise and experience.

We scheduled a post-course follow up meeting on <u>Friday, September 19</u> at <u>2:30 p.m.</u> at which I will share my reaction to the program, the most important insights and my specific goals for achievement based on what I learned.

Thanks again for your support.

Sincerely,

<u>Ralph</u>

COMPLETED EXAMPLE OF WORKSHEET 1.5
Preparation Planner

 **Do It Now**

Instructions: List all the preparatory assignments you have been asked to complete before the training and development program. Check them off as you complete them. In the comments area, jot down your immediate reaction to the value of the assignment and the key "takeaways."

✓	Due Date	Date Finished	Assignment	Comments and Takeaways
✓	8/15	8/12	Identify 360 feedback providers and ask them to participate	
✓	8/30	8/25	Complete and submit self-evaluation	Whew! Long, hard, and thought-provoking. , Not sure whether I was being too hard on myself or overly modest.
✓	9/15	9/10	Read first three chapters of *The Trusted Advisor*	Argues that technical competence is not enough/you have to earn personal trust to be an effective advisor.
☐	9/15		Meet with manager to discuss per-work and desired learning outcomes	
☐	9/15		Interview one key client about his or her concept of "trusted advisor"	

COMPLETED EXAMPLE OF WORKSHEET 1.6
Personal Challenge

Do It Now

Instructions: Read the description below. Choose a few new ways of interacting that you are going to experiment with during the training. Afterward, record your observations (results/reactions) and your intent (do more, do less) going forward.

Category	My Usual Response	I Am Going to Try	Result/Reaction	Plan Going Forward:
Questions/Team Reports	☐ Jump in with the answers	☐ Consciously wait to encourage others to participate		☐ Do more ☐ Do less ☐ Other:_____
	☑ Hang back and let others answer	☑ Force myself to volunteer answers more often	*Got some nice compliments on some of my insights and contributions*	☑ Do more ☐ Do less ☐ Other:_____
Role Play and Demonstrations	☐ Volunteer immediately; enjoy being in front of the group.	☐ Hang back, encourage others to have a turn		☐ Do more ☐ Do less ☐ Other:_____
	☑ Try my best not to be picked to demonstrate	☑ Force myself to volunteer to be one of the players	*Really hard; hated it. I think other people were happy I did, and I probably learned more than just watching*	☐ Do more ☐ Do less ☑ Other:_____ *Be selective; volunteer when I need to show leadership*
Teamwork and Group Exercises	☐ Step into the leadership role. Take charge; organize the work.	☐ Consciously encourage others to lead the group; practice followership		☐ Do more ☐ Do less ☐ Other:_____
	☑ Be a great team player and support whoever takes the lead, but don't lead myself.	☑ Step up to the leadership role; ask to lead if someone else is always taking charge.	*Volunteered in a couple cases to give the report out. Found I was irritated by people who always grab the marker.*	☑ Do more ☐ Do less ☐ Other:_____

COMPLETED EXAMPLE OF WORKSHEET 1.7
Interpersonal Connections

 **Do It Now**

Instructions

1. Try to meet at least three new people at the learning event (or people you know only by name or reputation). Spend enough time with them at breaks, meals, and so forth so that you can complete the connections table below.

2. In addition to each person's name, find out what his or her job is—not just the title, but what it entails. Help yourself connect with this person by linking his or her name to something interesting and personal—a hobby, a place the person has lived or traveled, an interesting experience he or she has had, etc.

3. Listen for something that you have in common—a common work experience, a favorite kind of food, place to visit, family background, anything that helps you connect.

4. Finally, think about a possible business connection—could he or she be a consultant, a potential employee, a resource, a collaborator, or play some other role? The point is not whether you ultimately pursue any one of these ideas, but to train yourself to always be on the lookout for such opportunities.

Complete the chart below for at least three new people:

Name	What does he/she do for a living?	Something interesting about him/her personally	Something the two of you have in common	Potential business connection with the person
Gordon Market	Supervisor, Manufacturing (responsible for total quality/Six Sigma)	Likes to travel to exotic places on his own/took motorcycle trip through Thailand last summer.	We both are interested in people and cultures outside our own.	Gordon really knows a lot about process control and quality that applies to all kinds of business processes. Could be helpful in improving our own dept's output.
Lillian Graves	Sales and marketing support (plans all the trade shows, major meetings, etc.)	She is on the state champion clog-dancing team/loves the coordination and teamwork needed to win.	We have both worked for other companies, which gives us a different and useful perspective.	She offered to help our event coordinator if we get stuck, since she has a great deal of experience.
Catherine Colbert	Instructional designer in the training group	She trained for the Olympic team in fencing until she hurt her shoulder.	We both love cats.	Catherine is also an expert presentation skills coach who would be willing to help my team improve their presentation skills or recommend others.

COMPLETED EXAMPLE OF WORKSHEET 1.8
Recap WIIFM

Do It Now

Instructions: At the end of each topic or segment of the course, take a few minutes to complete the table below.

Topic or Segment	Big "Aha" or Idea I Could Use	Benefit/Payoff
Situational Leadership	There is no one, universal best leadership method. The most effective method depends on the person's development level in a particular job. For some, a coaching style is not enough direction; for others it is too much.	This explains why some people seem to want more direction from me and others want less. If I can adapt my style, I will be more effectives and so will my direct reports.
Social Styles	People vary in the amount of detail and personal relationships they want. To be an effective sales person, I need to be able to read people's natural styles and adapt my presentations accordingly.	I will be more efficient and more effective if I can read people's preferences and adapt my style accordingly.

COMPLETED EXAMPLE OF WORKSHEET 1.9
Goals for Applying Learning

Do It Now

Instructions: If your program does not include a goal-setting exercise, complete the worksheet below. Select one to no more than three things you want to accomplish using the new knowledge and skills acquired in the program. Think through the first steps you need to take, potential barriers to progress, and what will help you achieve your objectives.

GOAL 1

In the next <u>12</u> (weeks/months), <u>I will improve my close rates by handling objections better</u> [specify what you will accomplish].

The benefit to me and the organization will be: <u>I will be more effective and efficient and we are</u> <u>more likely to hit our revenue targets (plus, of course, I get a bigger commission)</u> [explain the value].

Evidence of progress and success will include <u>Feedback from my manager during her observations</u> <u>of my sales calls and—ultimately—my close rates</u> [define the indicators of progress and measures of success].

Potential impediments to progress and my plans to minimize them include:

Potential Impediment	Plan to Mitigate or Remove
Mainly internal — my tendency to cave in when an objection is raised	Plan for the call in advance; anticipate possible objections and rehearse how I will deal with them.

Given the above, the most important help I will need to achieve these goals is:

Help Needed	From Whom
Feedback from my manager on how I am doing and suggestions for continued improvement	My sales manager

Test your goal against the following benchmarks:

☑ I have defined just one, two, or three key things to accomplish.

☑ They require that I use and practice newly acquired skills and knowledge.

☑ They are connected to my existing priorities; I am using work I have to do anyway as my "practice field."

☑ They are specific about what I will accomplish and when.

☑ They require some "stretch" but are achievable in the time allotted.

COMPLETED EXAMPLE OF WORKSHEET 1.10
Elevator Speech

 **Do It Now**

Instructions: Answer the four questions below. If time permits, practice your elevator speech with a partner.

1. The most important/striking/insightful/valuable (pick one) thing I learned was: *that failure to delegate is one of the leading causes of failure among new managers.*

2. I am going to capitalize on this learning by: *really focusing on improving my ability to delegate.*

3. The benefit for our organization will be: *I will have more time to work on strategic—rather than tactical—issues and the people who work with me will get new and potentially interesting assignments.*

4. I'll need the following help to make this happen: *remind me when you see me doing work that I could—and should—have delegated to someone else.*

COMPLETED EXAMPLE OF WORKSHEET 1.11
Post-Program Meeting

Do It Now

Instructions: Prepare to meet your manager soon after attending the program by adapting your elevator speech as suggested below.

As you know I attended the <u>Project Management</u> program on <u>January 15 to 18.</u>

Overall, I found it <u>very worthwhile, partly as a refresher for what I already knew, but also because it introduced me to some new concepts and approaches.</u>

The most valuable [thing I learned, ~~insight I gained, exercise we did, etc.~~] was: <u>how to deal with project members who are not meeting their commitments,</u> which [<u>was</u> / ~~was not~~] in line with the focus for my learning we discussed beforehand.

My goals for applying what I learned are:

1. <u>In the next ten weeks, I will use what I learned to deal head-on with one of the project members [KT] who is not pulling his weight and who is continually missing deadlines, so that we can get the project back on track. Indicators of my success will be that KT begins to be a full contributor or is replaced.</u>

I expect the benefit for our department to be <u>greater productivity, with more projects being brought in on time and on budget; as well as less internal conflict on the project team.</u>

The greatest challenges I see in achieving my objectives are <u>getting cooperation from individuals (and their managers) who are not in our department.</u>

Therefore, I will especially appreciate your help with: <u>interceding with other managers at your level if my own efforts are not successful.</u>

What suggestions do you have regarding my goals or plans?

COMPLETED EXAMPLE OF WORKSHEET 1.12
First Steps

 **Do It Now**

Instructions: Write down the first three things you need to do to get started on your goals. Do them. Then record the date completed and the results or lessons learned.

✓	Critical First Steps	Date Completed	Results and Learnings
✓	1. Thank the people who provided input on my 360 feedback, tell them what I am going to work on, and ask for feedforward	9/1/08	People seemed genuinely pleased and surprised that I took the time to follow up with them. The feedforward worked great; it was a way for them to express wishes about my behavior without being negative and I got some good ideas I would not have thought of myself.
✓	2. Review my learning, objectives, and plan with my manager	9/5/08	Useful discussion. Marion agreed with my goals and gave me some additional performance advice that I would not otherwise have had. It seems like my time management problem was apparent to everyone but me.
☐	3. Stop checking my emails first thing in the morning. Instead, make a list of the key things I have to accomplish that day, before I get bogged down in emails and correspondence. Keep this up for at least three weeks.		

COMPLETED EXAMPLE OF WORKSHEET 1.13
Plot Your Progress

Instructions: Every two weeks, plot your progress toward achieving your learning application goals using the chart below. Post the chart prominently in your work space.

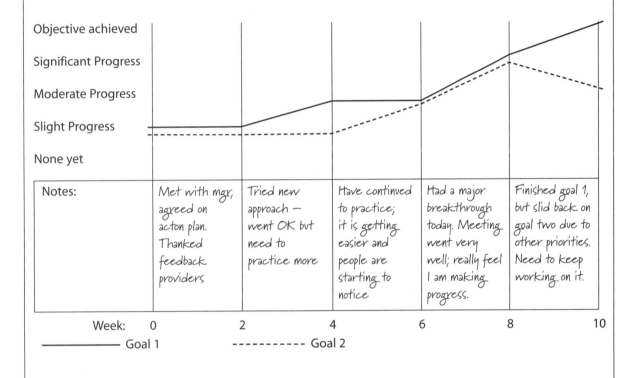

Objective achieved					
Significant Progress					
Moderate Progress					
Slight Progress					
None yet					
Notes:	Met with mgr, agreed on acton plan. Thanked feedback providers	Tried new approach — went OK but need to practice more	Have continued to practice; it is getting easier and people are starting to notice	Had a major breakthrough today. Meeting went very well; really feel I am making progress.	Finished goal 1, but slid back on goal two due to other priorities. Need to keep working on it.
Week:	0	2	4	6	8	10

———————— Goal 1   - - - - - - - - - - Goal 2

COMPLETED EXAMPLE OF WORKSHEET 1.14
Sources of Support

Do It Now

Instructions: Check the sources of support that you think will be of most interest/value to you personally, given your goals and job responsibilities.

Plan to Use	Source	What I hope to get from this source:
☑	My manager	Advice on better decision making; how she weighs choices and avoids "paralysis by analysis." I will ask her to critique the way I approached a recent decision as a means of learning.
☑	A fellow participant Who? Steven Frotheringale	Steven was the clearest thinker in our group about decision making and had a wealth of experience. We agreed to keep in touch; I'll reach out to him for an impartial view when I am struggling with a decision.
☐	Another colleague Who? _____	
☑	Reading Title: Getting to Yes	I want to learn more about "principled negotiation."
☐	Online materials Which? _____	
☑	Course materials Specifically: The section on decision making and the RACI model.	A refresher on the RACI model to help decide who needs to be involved versus just kept informed.
☐	A subject-matter expert Who? _____	
☐	A course instructor Who? _____	
☑	My direct reports	I want to both teach and learn with my direct reports by conducting "after-action reviews" of how we handled team decisions.

COMPLETED EXAMPLE OF WORKSHEET 1.15
Close the Loop

Instructions: Use this worksheet to help you plan a final meeting with your manager to "close the loop" on this round of development and to plan for the future.

Program you attended: *Parts and Service Department Management*

Date: *January 5–9, 2009*

What you consider your most important achievement or improvement that resulted from your attendance and follow-through:

Although the final results are not in, we have seen a significant increase in upselling accessories while at the same time increasing customer satisfaction scores. We will continue to track over the coming months.

Specific examples/evidence:

Accessory sales in the two months since I attended the training are up 13 percent (see sales report). Simultaneously, the monthly customer net promoter scores are up 8 percent compared to the same period last year and 10 percent compared to the monthly average.

What do you think you should work on next? [List three things that—if you could do them even faster, better, and more effectively—would make you even more valuable than you are today. In some cases, the most important thing will be to sustain, extend, or deepen the capabilities and skills you developed in this round.]

1. *Deepening understanding of the drivers of profitability and satisfaction among my team.*
2. *Increasing my own understanding of cost control and margin management.*
3. *Improving my ability to give feedback to my direct reports.*

Seek your manager's agreement with your achievements and plan for future development. Ask for her/his ideas on the best opportunities to continue to learn and improve your performance.

Getting Your Money's Worth

········ **for Participants** ········

1 Get Ready

- Get clear about what YOU want
- Get your manager's agreement
- Get the preparation done

2 Get Engaged

- Get your head in the game
- Get out of your comfort zone
- Get connected
- Get specific
- Get your story straight

3 Get Results

- Get reconnected
- Get going
- Get help
- Get better
- Get ready to do it again

Getting Your Money's Worth from Training and Development

A Guide to Breakthrough
Learning for Managers

Andrew McK. Jefferson

Roy V.H. Pollock

Calhoun W. Wick

Pfeiffer

A Wiley Imprint
www.pfeiffer.com

Published by Pfeiffer
A Wiley Imprint
989 Market Street, San Francisco, CA 94103-1741
www.pfeiffer.com

For additional copies/bulk purchases of this book in the U.S. please contact 800-274-4434.

Pfeiffer books and products are available through most bookstores. To contact Pfeiffer directly call our
Customer Care Department within the U.S. at 800-274-4434, outside the U.S. at 317-572-3985, fax 317-572-4002,
or visit www.pfeiffer.com.

Pfeiffer also publishes its books in a variety of electronic formats. Some content that appears in print may not
be available in electronic books.

ISBN 978-0-470-41112-4

Acquiring Editor: Matthew Davis
Marketing Manager: Brian Grimm
Production Editor: Michael Kay
Editor: Rebecca Taff
Manufacturing Supervisor: Becky Morgan
Editorial Assistant: Lindsay Morton
Interior Composition: Stan Shoptaugh
Illustrations: Lotus Art

Printed in the United States of America
Printing   10 9 8 7 6 5 4 3 2 1

Contents

List of Inserts

Contents of the Website

Results Readiness Scorecards

Job Aids

More Frequently Asked Questions

More "Who Says So?"

Case Studies

More Sample Worksheets

Additional Tips and Guides

Learn More

A Guide to Breakthrough Learning for Managers

How to Use This Book

This book is a practical "how-to" guide. It provides efficient, succinct, proven procedures for getting the greatest value from training and development of your direct reports. It is short because it is not that hard to get a big return on training—provided you and your direct reports do the work necessary. Like so many other things in life, you get out pretty much what you put in. No investment, no return.

Getting your money's worth from training will require some (but not a lot) of your time. The steps we recommend are designed to achieve significant impact while making efficient use of your time. The whole process will require about three hours of your time over the next three months—approximately fifteen minutes a week. The time you invest will be repaid many times over in terms of greater productivity and higher quality work from those who report to you.

To save you time, we have separated the "need to know" from the "nice to know." The actions you need to take to maximize value ("How?") are set in this typeface on a white background. If you are by nature a driver, somebody who just wants to "get 'er done," or is short of time, read only the non-shaded pages and complete the tasks labeled 🖉 Do It Now . There are completed examples in the appendix.

Tick them off as you complete them on the checklist inside the front cover. To help guide you, there are completed examples of each worksheet in the appendix (page 49). Optional readings ("Why?") are set in a different typeface on gray backgrounds. If you are by nature analytical, curious about the research behind the recommendations, or skeptical about the advice in self-help books, then read the 🔼 Who Says So? sections that summarize the evidence. Specific suggestions and more detailed guidance are denoted by the 👤 GuideMe® icon. Answers to frequently asked questions ❓ FAQs are also provided.

The flip side of this book is a guide for participants on getting *their* money's worth from training. It defines the specific actions a learner needs to take before, during, and after training to maximize the performance impact.

We suggest you quickly review the checklists, worksheets, and advice your direct report has been given. You will also find the participant part of this book valuable when you are scheduled to attend a training or development program yourself.

Introduction to the Guide for Managers

Know-how and expertise are the new drivers of business success.

In the Industrial Age, investments in fixed assets—plants, buildings, and equipment—were the main source of competitive advantage. Today, competitive advantage derives mainly from human capital—the skills, know-how, creativity, and performance of employees. Growth in corporate profitability has been fueled mainly by greater productivity of *human capital* for the past twenty-five years (Echols, 2008). Indeed, traditional capital assets now account for only about 20 percent of the book value of most companies, even less in high-tech or service industries.

Remaining competitive and profitable in today's rapidly evolving business climate requires investing to continuously upgrade employees' knowledge, skills, and performance. Training and development are vital. But training alone rarely improves performance.

That's where you come in.

Training doesn't miraculously lead to results. Managers have a critical role in making sure that investments in learning and development pay off.

You have been provided with a copy of this book because someone who reports to you is scheduled to attend a training and development program. It might be a program you recommended, one he or she asked to attend, or one mandated by the company. You might be enthusiastic about your direct report's attendance, skeptical about its value, or even irritated about the time it will consume.

"I think you should be more explicit here in step two."

It doesn't matter. You need to make the most of it.

The investment is going to be made in any case. It is up to you, as manager, to make sure that the training pays a dividend. What *you* do (or *don't do*) as a manager has tremendous impact on whether the training adds value or is wasted (see Who Says So?). By completing the steps in this workbook, you can ensure that you, your employee, and the company get their money's worth.

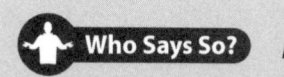 **Who Says So?**   *Managers Determine Training Success or Failure*

Studies at Pfizer dramatically illustrate how much managers influence the outcome of training and development.

Several months after a leadership development program, 360-degree assessments were repeated and compared to pre-program results. The training worked—provided that managers were actively engaged in the process.

Participants showed statistically significant gains on all five of the five most-frequent development needs *as long as their managers were actively involved during the post-course period.* In contrast, participants *in the same program* whose managers were not actively involved during the post-course showed no performance improvement or made much smaller gains than those who had manager support (Stewart, 2007).

Same kind of participants, same program, same content, but dramatically different results, depending on whether or not the manager was engaged. In short, managers matter.

A recent study at American Express also underscored the impact of managers on training effectiveness (American Express, 2007). Three months after training, participants were classified into groups based on the extent of improvement. High-improvement participants—those who achieved significantly better results post-training—were *four times* more likely to have had conversations with their manager about how to apply the learning than those who achieved little or no improvement. Other measures of managerial support were all significantly greater in the high-improvement group.

The study authors concluded:

> *"The true impact of a training program will best be predicted by the work environment participants return to after the event. More specifically, this refers to the type of leader they work with and report to after their respective training."*

The harsh reality is this: *Lack of manager involvement is the most common reason that training fails to produce improved performance.*

It is true, of course, that even in well-managed companies there are some training programs that are poorly targeted, badly designed, or ineffectively delivered. But they are not the main problem. "An immediate leader has the potential to either make or break any training effort (American Express, 2007)."

If training fails to add value, you bear much of the responsibility.

 **Who Says So?**   *Managers Are a Common Cause of Training Failure*

Corporate training professionals estimate that, on average, only 16 percent of participants in training and development programs transfer their learning to their jobs in a way that improves performance (Wick, Jefferson, & Pollock, 2008). *Failure of supervisors* to encourage and reinforce application of the training on the job is the most commonly cited factor that inhibits learning transfer (Foxon, 1993).

A Motorola Inc. study found that plants in which quality improvement training was reinforced by senior management realized a $33 return on every dollar invested (Wiggenhorn, 1990). In contrast, plants that provided the same training but without management follow-up produced a *negative* return on investment.

Further evidence that managers' lack of involvement will cause otherwise successful courses (and participants) to fail include the studies by Pfizer and American Express cited above and a Xerox Inc. study that found a paltry 13 percent of skills were retained by trainees six months after training *if managers failed to provide coaching and support* as the skills were being applied (Clemmer, 2008).

Bottom line: Your active interest in the impact of training has a positive effect on the outcome; your indifference or neglect will undermine otherwise successful programs.

"My end of the boat didn't leak!"

In other words, YOU are the single most important determinant of whether or not the company gets its money's worth from training and development. As manager, you set the tone, you influence what gets done and what is ignored, what is rewarded and what is considered a waste of time.

The buck stops with you: If you are not actively engaged in helping your employees use the training to improve their performance, then you can't blame the training department or human resources or your direct reports if the training fails to pay dividends.

What's in It for You?

Why should you invest your time and energy following up on your direct reports' training, when you already have more work than you can possibly do? What's in it for you?

You benefit when your employees' performance improves—which is the reason for investing in training and development in the first place. You need to have a strong, competent, high-caliber team working for you if you want to get ahead—to continue to succeed and advance in your career. The better they are, the better for you.

 **FAQs**   *Isn't That Training's Responsibility?*

Why do I have to get involved in making sure training pays a dividend? Isn't that the responsibility of the training department?

When performance doesn't improve after training—especially if the training was expensive or was introduced with a great deal of fanfare—then there is a lot of finger-pointing about Why It Didn't Work and a hunt for Who's to Blame?

It is like two people in a boat that just sank arguing about whose end leaked the most. They are both in the water; the only ones who will benefit from their internal squabbling are the competitors (the sharks).

It takes a partnership to produce performance improvement. Training cannot do it without managerial support, because the training department does not control work assignments, priorities, or rewards for your direct reports; nor would you want them to. At the same time, you need training's expertise in learning design, delivery, and execution.

When training succeeds, everyone wins and deserves to share in the credit. When training fails, everyone loses and everyone owns some of the blame.

"George Tully is a really first-rate individual, up from second-rate this past quarter"

When you gain a reputation as someone who is good at developing people, then the best people want to work for you. If you have top-notch direct reports who can step into your role, then you can be promoted to higher levels of responsibility.

You also want to be seen as someone who makes good use of employees' time and company resources, someone who extracts maximum value from each opportunity. The more value you create from the resources entrusted to you, the more resources will be entrusted to you.

Bottom line: It is in your own self-interest, as well as that of the company and the people who work for you, to make sure you get your money's worth whenever one of your direct reports participates in training.

And the best part is that helping your direct reports achieve their full potential is one of the most satisfying and personally-rewarding things you can do as a leader. Nothing delights us (the authors) more than seeing people whom we have mentored go on to satisfying and successful careers of

their own. We think it is a hallmark of a true leader. It is not only the right thing to do, but rewarding as well. Try it; you'll like it.

Everyone Can Improve

Even if the direct report who is scheduled for training is already your top performer, he or she can still get better. The world's best business leaders, athletes, actors, artists, and professionals never stop trying to improve. Competition demands it. No one is ever so good that he or she cannot still get better (or get beaten).

Think about the performance of the direct report who is scheduled for training. In Worksheet 2.1, list three things that, if he or she could do them faster, better, or more effectively, would make him or her even more valuable.

WORKSHEET 2.1
Improvement Opportunities

Do It Now

Instructions: List three things that your direct report could do faster, better, or more effectively that would make him or her even more valuable to your organization:

1. _____

_____

2. _____

_____

3. _____

_____

The Three Keys to Getting Your Money's Worth as a Manager

A manager must do three key things to extract the maximum value from the training and development of his or her employees:

1. Be more up-front.
2. Be more engaged.
3. Be more results-driven.

1. Be More Up-Front

Being more up-front means getting involved *before* the training starts. You may be surprised to learn that research shows a manager's actions *prior to the training* have a significant influence on the value realized *afterward*. To optimize results, take the following actions up-front:

☐ Do your homework.

☐ Meet with your direct report(s).

☐ Make your expectations clear.

☐ Schedule follow-up and accountability.

Do Your Homework

To make the best use of the opportunity, you need to do a little homework before the program begins.

First, find out what is going on. If you want to get your money's worth from training and development, you have to know what's going on—what the program entails, what business purpose it serves, and what topics are covered.

The training and development department should send you this information in advance, or make it easily available to you online. If you don't already have the information you need, ask for it, and make the point that since managers share responsibility for making sure training pays off, they have to know what is going on. You should not have to go hunting for the information you need to fulfill your role–especially since the training department's success depends on you.

 **FAQs**

What If I Think the Training Will Not Be Productive?

There may be times when you feel strongly that the training will be a waste of time and money. What you do about it depends on why you feel the way you do and on who is driving the request for training.

If the employee initiated the request to attend, then you need to express your reservations about the value of the program. It may be that your direct report is already skilled in the area and won't learn enough new to warrant the time and expense. It may be that you have experience with the program—having attended it yourself or having sent other employees—and found it of limited value. If you choose to discourage your direct report from taking a program that he or she requested, be prepared to suggest a more valuable learning experience—a different program or a developmental assignment—so the person does not feel you are just trying to stifle his or her development.

If the program is mandated by management, HR, Legal, or Regulatory Affairs, then you have a different problem. If all the feedback you have received suggests that the program lacks substance or relevance, then you need to take your case to the training department and/or senior management. Time is such a precious commodity these days that no company can afford to waste it. As a leader, you owe it to the people who report to you to plead their case against poorly conceived, -designed, or -delivered programs. Be prepared to defend your concerns with specific examples and to offer constructive suggestions or alternatives.

In the meantime, counsel your direct reports to make the most of the opportunity by networking with other departments, practicing their leadership skills, and so forth (see the participant's guide, page 19). Be careful not to be overly negative about the program to your direct reports, or your concerns about a lack of value will become a self-fulfilling prophecy.

If the program is one that your direct report asked to attend outside your own organization, then he or she is responsible for providing you with the rationale for attendance and the course objectives, content, and agenda. If this has not been done, ask for the information now.

Scan the course material looking for the most valuable topics and exercises based on the performance improvement opportunities you identified for your direct report in Worksheet 2.1. Then complete the WIIFM worksheet 2.2 below.

WORKSHEET 2.2
WIIFM for Managers

Do It Now

Direct Report's Name: _____

Name of Program: _____

Date of Program: _____

Instructions for Managers

1. In the first column, write two to five bullet points that summarize the key deliverables for your unit. Why does your group exist? How does your group create value for the business? This step is important; training and development must ultimately support the organization's objectives.

2. In column 2, write out the specific results for which your direct report is personally responsible. Ideally, these should mesh with her/his annual performance goals.

3. Refer to Worksheet 2.1. No matter how good your direct report is, he or she can get better at something, either to do the current job better or to prepare for greater responsibility. What do the top performers, the best of the best, in the field do better than your direct report can do currently? List the best opportunities for improvement in this column.

4. Look at the course description and objectives. What does it cover that is relevant to this employee? What does it promise? [If you don't know, find out.]

5. Put columns 3 and 4 together to fill in column 5. What do you want your direct report to do better and differently as a result of attending the program that will improve his or her personal performance and that of your department?

6. Review your completed WIIFM Worksheet with your direct report. He or she should have completed one independently (Worksheet 1.2). Compare notes and perceptions.

7. Agree on the top learning objectives for the forthcoming program.

	1. Most important deliverables of our business/ organizational unit	2. Most important results for which this person is responsible	3. What new or improved skills/ knowledge would help him/her deliver better results	4. Relevant topics covered in the training or development program	5. What I want him/her to do better or differently afterward to improve performance
Your Input					

In the participant's guide, we encouraged your direct report to complete a similar WIIFM Worksheet (participant's guide, page 11) and to schedule a meeting with you to discuss it. Comparing your worksheets is a great way to check for alignment around responsibilities, deliverables, developmental needs, and priorities for improvement. It affords you an opportunity to supply always-valuable performance coaching. A recommended structure and tips for getting the most from the discussion are provided in the GuideMe on page 16.

> *A pre-training discussion is one of the single most important things you can do to be sure that both you and your direct report get your money's worth.*

If your direct report has not already scheduled a pre-training meeting with you, schedule one now.

Keep your end of the bargain. Holding your direct reports accountable for using what they are taught is vital to getting your money's worth from training. To do so credibly, however, you must first model the behavior. Be sure to hold up your end of the bargain with respect to completing preparatory work and providing support.

If you are asked to provide input (360-degree feedback, etc.) as part of the learning experience, provide it thoughtfully and on time. By the same token, make the time to meet with your direct report to discuss his or her development, no matter how busy you are. Nothing sends a stronger message that "you are not important" to employees than when their manager is "too busy" to invest time in their development. Employees who feel their manager does not care about their development are *five times* more likely to quit than those who feel their company is committed to helping them learn and grow.

> *People don't quit companies, they quit their managers.*

No one questions how incredibly busy you are or how many pressing deadlines you have. But that is no excuse; developing people is one of the

most important—perhaps *the* most important—tasks of a manager. It is also critical to your personal success.

So carve out the time to complete whatever preparation is needed. Do it thoughtfully and candidly. This is not the time to pull punches; resist the urge to just tick the "middle of the road" ratings. If you feel that your direct report is falling seriously short in some areas, this is a great time to say so. It is also a great opportunity to highlight areas in which he or she excels and encourage your report to build on his or her strengths.

 **Who Says So?**   *Pre-Training Discussions Are Important*

There is good evidence that training yields better results when managers and their direct reports meet beforehand. Brinkerhoff and Montesino (1995) found that participants who had discussions with their managers before and after training achieved significantly higher levels of skill application than people who attended the same programs but did not have these conversations.

Professional trainers acknowledge how important a role you play in setting expectations. Broad and Newstrom (1992) asked trainers to rank the relative impact of nine role-time combinations on learning transfer. Trainers rated a before-training meeting between a manager and his or her direct reports as having *greater impact* on learning transfer than their own role during the training!

By meeting with your direct report before training, you underscore the importance you place on getting a return for the time and money that will be invested, and you help your direct report focus on the most valuable elements of the program.

Meet with Your Direct Report(s)

Meet with your direct report—ideally in person, but at least by phone—before the upcoming training. It needn't be a long meeting—fifteen to twenty minutes should suffice—but it needs to happen if you want to get the most from the opportunity.

Surprisingly, managers have their greatest impact on learning outcomes *before* the training program. (See "Who Says So?") That's because talking to your direct reports before the training establishes *learning intentionality*. It helps them focus, makes it clear that you place value on the investment, sets expectations for application and results, establishes a timeline for follow-through, and spells out the definition for success.

A recommended agenda is given in GuideMe below.

 **GuideMe®**   *Pre-Training Meeting Plan*

Agenda: [Plan for a 15-to-20 minute discussion.]

1. Review direct report's top three developmental opportunities.

2. Compare to your list and discuss any major differences.

3. Review direct report's WIIFM (What's in It for Me) worksheet.

4. Compare your answers; discuss points of agreement and differences.

5. Agree on the most important learning opportunities.

6. Commemorate the agreement in a learning contract or brief memorandum.

Detailed Coaching Guide

1. "What do you see as your three best opportunities to further improve your performance?" [Write them down as direct report describes them.]

   A. Why those three in particular? [Listen to rationale.]

   B. Share the three you had written down.

      i. If you are in agreement: "I am pleased that we picked very much the same things. Let's see how we can use this course to further your career." [Move on to WIIFM worksheet.]

      ii. If you are not in agreement, then talk about differences. The choices include:

      "I did not put this one on my list because I feel that it is already a strength for you."

      "I agree that this one you listed would also be good to improve, but I think this other one is more important because …."

      "You know, I agree that this item on your list is more important than this one on mine, so let's focus on the one you chose."

2. "Let's look at the WIIFM worksheet."

   A. Read your direct report's answers.

   B. Compare them with how you answered.

   C. Start by pointing out the areas in which there is substantial agreement.

   D. If your direct report's answers are quite different from yours, coach by asking, "Help me understand why you listed…." Then listen actively to the answer. Be willing to accept a different answer than your own if it is justifiable or perhaps better than yours.

3. Given the above, agree on one to three (no more) of the most important things for your direct report to take away from the course.

4. Ask your direct report to complete the learning contract or to send you a brief email summarizing the discussion.

5. Schedule a short meeting with your direct report as soon as possible after the training to hear a report on the program and his or her goals and plans for implementation.

Make Your Expectations Clear

Put a stake in the ground. In your pre-training discussion, make it clear that you consider training an important investment and that you expect to see application and improvement as a result.

Set your expectations high, because expectations tend to be self-fulfilling prophesies; people rise (or fall) to the occasion. An appropriately challenging sales budget yields higher revenues than an easily achieved one. High expectations for performance produce greater effort than low (or no) expectations. Employees excel more often when expectations are high and clear.

When you express confidence that your direct report's performance will improve after training, it is more likely to improve than when you—intentionally or unintentionally—telegraph low expectations for the outcome. One reason that managers are often disappointed with the results of training and development is that they themselves set the bar too low in terms of expected improvement.

Agree on objectives and the definition of success. Close the meeting by agreeing on deliverables, just as you would for any other business objective.

Have your direct report summarize the meeting either as a formal learning contract (Exhibit 2.1) or as a less formal memorandum (Exhibit 2.2). Suggested formats are provided in the participant's guide. Whatever form the summary takes, be sure the results of the meeting and your (high) expectations are recorded—and tracked—with the same rigor that you document other business objectives and investments.

Learning objectives are business objectives
and should be managed as such.

Even if you have a close and informal working relationship with your direct report, follow the process and commemorate the agreement; it is good discipline that will avoid potential misunderstanding and will yield better results.

Exhibit 2.1

Sample Learning Contract

In order to maximize the value of my learning and development in the upcoming <u>Parts Department Management</u> program, I agree to:

☑ Complete all required pre-course reading and other assignments

☑ Attend and be actively engaged in all sessions

☑ Develop goals for applying what I learned to my work

☑ Execute a follow-through plan that improves my performance

☑ Report the results

☑ Share highlights and insights with my co-workers

☑ <u>Seek out and bring back Best Practices from other dealerships</u>

Specifically, I will focus on <u>inventory management</u> during the program in order to improve <u>my ability to maximize profitability and efficiency of repair process</u> afterward.

Signed: <u>Malcolm Rogers</u>

Date: <u>July 23, 2009</u>

MANAGER'S AGREEMENT

As the manager of the employee above, I agree to:

1. Attend and participate in any advance briefing sessions for supervisors

2. Meet with my direct report before the program to discuss the most important developmental opportunities the training provides

3. Release my direct report from sufficient work assignments that he/she has time to complete the preparation for the training and attend all the sessions

4. Minimize interruptions during the training

5. Meet again after the program to discuss the highlights of the session and mutually explore opportunities for application

6. Model the desired behaviors for the trainee

7. Provide encouragement, support, and reinforcement for efforts to apply the training

8. Provide specific opportunities for my direct report to practice the new behaviors and skills

9. Provide suggestions for continued development

Our post-course follow-up meeting is scheduled for: <u>Friday, September 19th</u>

Signed: <u>Maria Garcia</u>

Date: <u>July 25, 2009</u>

Exhibit 2.2

Sample Completed Learning Memorandum

Dear Margaret,

Thank you for meeting with me today to discuss the upcoming Leader to Leader Program.

We agreed that the most important thing for me to focus on during the course was improving my ability to communicate a compelling vision that others want to contribute to and make happen in order to improve my performance in the area of leadership and team building.

You agreed to make sure that I had the time to do the assignments, attend the program with minimum interruptions, and have opportunities to practice my new skills / knowledge afterward. You also agreed to provide coaching so that I can benefit from your expertise and experience.

We scheduled a post-course follow up meeting on Friday, September 19 at 2:30 p.m. at which I will share my reaction to the program, the most important insights and my specific goals for achievement based on what I learned.

Thanks again for your support.

Sincerely,

Ralph

If you do not receive a summary of the meeting from your direct report in a day or two, ask for it again.

If you still do not receive a clear statement of learning intent, you have two choices: If the training is optional, you could deny attendance. That would send a very clear message about how seriously you take the investment in training. Indeed, some companies have made a learning contract essential for admission and have sent people home who turned up without one. You only have to do that once for people to get the message.

If the training is required, but you have not received a completed learning contract, send a memorandum that expresses your displeasure that the employee did not fulfill this obligation and that reinforces your expectation for follow-through (see Worksheet 2.3).

WORKSHEET 2.3
Learning Memorandum

 **Do It Now**

Instructions: Complete and send this memorandum only if you have not received a meeting summary from your direct report and the training is mandatory.

Dear _____,

We met the other day to discuss the upcoming _____ program. I am very disappointed that I have not received the summary of that discussion that I asked you to pre-pare. I hope this is not indicative of the effort you will put into preparing and following up on your education. If so, I am concerned about the wisdom of investing in your development.

We agreed that the most important thing for you to focus on during the course was _____ _____ in order to improve your performance in the areas of _____ _____.

You agreed to do all the assignments, give the program your full attention, and practice your new skills/knowledge afterward. We scheduled a post-course follow-up meeting on _____ _____ at _____, at which I will ask you to share your reaction to the program, your most important insights, and your specific goals for improving your performance.

I expect—and look forward to seeing—you apply what you learn to improve your performance.

Sincerely,

_____

Plan Ahead

Now is also a good time to start thinking about the post-program period. Specifically:

1. How will you create opportunities for your direct reports to practice what they learn immediately after the training?

2. What will success look like?

3. How will you assess whether their performance has improved?

4. If their performance has improved, what will you do to recognize and reward it?

You do not need definitive answers to these questions at the moment, but you will get greater return on the training investment if you start thinking about them in advance.

Schedule Follow-Up and Accountability

Last—but by no means, least—schedule a specific time to meet or talk again after the learning experience—the sooner the better.

Nothing else underscores your interest and intention to provide follow-up support and accountability as much as setting a firm date to discuss the program, what was learned, and your direct report's plans for implementation.

Resist the urge to say, "Let's schedule something when you get back." Set a firm date to meet in the first week after the program and make every effort to keep it. If you cancel the meeting or reschedule it repeatedly, you send a clear, if unintended, message that you really don't give a damn, and much of training's potential value will be wasted. (See FAQ: "What If I Don't Really Give a Damn?")

 **FAQs** *What If I Really Don't Give a Damn?*

The fundamental premise of this workbook is that you care about whether you get a return on the training investment in your direct report. But suppose you don't?

Then you need to think about why you don't give a damn and decide on an appropriate course of action.

If you don't give a damn because you think this particular training is a waste of time, then you have a leadership responsibility to take up the issue with the training department or senior management, rather than remain silent and have your employees continue to waste their time.

If you don't give a damn because you have written this employee off as a chronic low performer who isn't worth investing in, then you have a leadership responsibility to do your department—and the employee—a favor by replacing him or her with a more capable individual. Perform one last reality check before you do, however: Have you given this person unambiguous performance feedback? Have you made a serious effort to coach to improved performance? If the answer to both these questions is yes, then pull the plug.

Or maybe you don't give a damn because you are overloaded with work and don't believe your impact warrants making it a priority. In that case, read the evidence (Who Says So?) about how much influence managers have on getting a return on investment. Then think about the value that could be created by fulfilling this important managerial responsibility instead of some less important task.

2. Be More Engaged

When it comes to getting value from training and development, *you* are the most important leader in your organization. That's because your direct reports look to you for direction. You set the tone:

> "If you're a manager in an organization, to *your* direct reports *you* are the *most important* leader in your organization. *You* are more likely than any other leader to influence their desire to stay or leave, the trajectory of their careers, their ethical behavior, their ability to perform at their best, their drive to wow customers, their satisfaction with their jobs, and their motivation to share the organization's vision and values."
>
> —Kouzes & Posner, 2007, p. 338

If you show an active interest in your direct reports' development, so will they. They'll devote greater effort to apply what they learned over a longer period. As a result, they'll improve their performance faster and to a greater degree. You, they, and your department will benefit.

The three keys to effective engagement are:

☐ Just ask.

☐ Create opportunities.

☐ Provide feedback and encouragement.

Just Ask

The old adage goes: "What gets inspected gets respected."

One of the most powerful and inexpensive performance tools a manager has is simply showing interest. What a manager attends to, his or her direct reports attend to. When you ask your direct reports about the program, what they learned, and what progress they are making, you telegraph that you consider it to be important. Once your direct reports realize you consider it to be important, so will they; they will give learning transfer greater attention and effort, and so achieve better results.

A key to getting better results is to "Just Ask."

Showing interest doesn't require a lot of time, paperwork, or meetings. Brief conversations in the hall or cafeteria will have the desired effect. Better yet, practice MBWA (management by wandering around); stop by your direct report's work area and ask *en passent*.

As noted above, the most important time to "just ask" is before the training. The second most important time is immediately afterward.

Why? Because knowledge is most fragile when it is new; the forgetting curve is steepest at the beginning. When you "just ask" about the training afterward, your employee has to retrieve and reprocess the experience, which facilitates its subsequent recall and application. Guidelines for the first post-training conversation are given in the next GuideMe.

 **GuideMe®**   *Post-Training Discussion*

Overview

1. Schedule a post-training follow-up discussion as soon as practical after the training program.

2. Plan for a twenty-to thirty-minute discussion. Having the conversation is more important than its length; even ten to fifteen minutes will underscore your interest and improve learning transfer.

3. Spend most of your time listening and asking questions. Your direct report should do most of the talking.

   Ask four key questions:

   • What was most valuable to you?

   • What are your goals for applying what you learned?

   • How will achieving your goals benefit the department and your career?

   • What support do you need to achieve them?

The objectives of the conversation are to underscore your interest, encourage your direct report to reflect on the experience (thereby reinforcing it), and get his or her commitment to practice the new knowledge and skills to achieve a valuable outcome.

Detailed Coaching Guide

1. Meet and greet. Thank the person for meeting with you. Express your interest in hearing about the program and how he or she plans to apply it.

2. Ask: "What was most valuable to you?"

   • Listen carefully to the answer.

   • Play back what you heard to be sure you understood: "So, for you, the most valuable part of attending was...."

   • Ask for further clarification or amplification to help your direct report cement his or her understanding and practice critical thinking. "Tell me a little more about that ...." or "Do you think that other people found different parts to be the most valuable, and if so, why?"

3. Your direct report should have *one to three* strong, written goals for applying the program's content. If you have not already received them, ask: "What are your goals for applying what you learned?"

   • Review the goals (if you have not already).

   • Do they focus on the right things? Do the goals relate to responsibilities the person already has? Are they sufficiently challenging (stretch)?

   • If not, ask questions: "Why did you choose this particular area to focus on?" "Can you think of anything else that could be a higher priority or more valuable?"

   • If you agree with the goals, move on to the benefit question. If not, provide guidance: "I'd like to see you be clearer about the outcomes" or "I'd like to rewrite the second goal to focus more on _____ because that is where I see the greatest opportunity for you to improve your performance," etc.

4. Ask: "How will achieving these goals benefit the department and your career?"
    - If the program does not require participants to define the "so what?" as part of the goal, ask your direct report to explain the value of each objective.
    - Help your direct report focus on benefits to be sure he or she has picked the most valuable goals and to increase commitment to achieving them.
5. Ask: "What support/opportunities do you need to achieve them?"
    - Show your support by giving your direct report the opportunity to ask for resources, time, or projects to help achieve his or her goals.
    - If these are reasonable, provide them.
    - If the request is more than it is possible for you to grant, then explain the limitations and, if necessary, revise the goal to be achievable with the resources and time at your disposal.
6. Finally, set a specific time for follow-up (if a schedule has not already been established by the program's use of a follow-through management system). "I'd like to see a progress report on [Date]."

Asking about the training once is better than nothing. But to truly improve performance requires sustained effort over time.

All the research on human performance indicates that deliberate practice is more important than "natural talent" (see "Who Says So?"). For someone to become really good at anything, they have to do it over and over, reflecting on their performance each time and getting coaching and feedback along the way.

Improvement Requires Deliberate Practice

Writing in *Fortune* magazine, Geoffrey Colvin summarized the research on "What It Takes to Be Great" this way: "The evidence, scientific as well as anecdotal, is overwhelmingly in favor of deliberate practice as the source of great performance."

In other words, getting really good at anything, requires practice—and lots of it. A one-day or even several-week training program is not going to have a lasting effect on performance unless it is reinforced with deliberate practice, coaching, and feedback. Ericsson, a leading researcher on peak performance, defines deliberate practice as "considerable, specific, and sustained efforts to do something you *can't* do well (Ericsson, Prietula, & Cokely, 2007).

But how do you practice business? Colvin suggests that it is "all about how you do what you're already doing—you create the practice in your work …going at any task with a new goal: Instead of merely trying to get it done, you aim to get better at it."

Ericsson stresses the importance of coaches and coaching in performance improvement. "The development of expertise requires coaches who are capable of giving constructive, even painful feedback." Studies in many fields of human performance—from business to chess grand masters—confirms these findings (Ross, 2006).

In other words, training can play an important role in catalyzing and accelerating development, but learning becomes improved performance only through practice over time with ongoing coaching. That explains why managers have such profound impact on the success or failure of corporate education.

"Sometimes it's important to stop whatever break you're taking and just do the work."

So, to maximize training's value, find ways to encourage continued practice and sustain your direct report's focus and efforts. Set up a formal schedule for assessing progress and results (see "Be More Results-Driven" below) and remember to "just ask" now and then about progress on learning objectives.

Create Opportunities

The second critical way that managers facilitate performance improvement following training is by creating opportunities.

As manager, you exert control over workflow, assignments, and resources. Use these prerogatives to create opportunities for your direct reports to continue to learn and to practice newly acquired skills and knowledge on the job.

Start by creating a high-quality opportunity to learn in the first place.

☐ Encourage employees to attend developmentally appropriate training.

☐ Minimize interruptions and distractions when they do, so that they can truly attend to, not merely attend, the training.

☐ After training, assign specific projects, tasks, or other responsibilities that will require your direct reports to practice their new knowledge and abilities.

Encourage the Right Kind of Training

Developmentally appropriate training, combined with managed follow-through, will reward your department with dividends that far exceed the time and money invested.

The key phrase above, however, is *developmentally appropriate.* The training must be relevant to the person's current or future role and include skills, content, models, and approaches they have not already mastered. It is a waste of time to send people to training in areas in which they already excel; that they won't be able to use in the foreseeable future; or for which they have insufficient background knowledge and experience.

Likewise, training will not improve performance when the root causes are poor motivation, unclear expectations, inadequate feedback, or lack of recognition and reward, although it is often misused to try to solve such issues.

Free Up the Time to Learn

Effective learning requires undivided attention. As a manager, you can increase the amount of learning that takes place by relieving your direct reports as much as possible from day-to-day responsibilities during training so that they can truly concentrate on learning.

Have someone else "cover" for them, take their calls, or otherwise handle as many of their responsibilities as possible. Adjust due dates of their projects if necessary and resist the urge to contact them yourself during the training unless absolutely necessary.

Encourage trainees themselves to stay focused. Discourage them from calling their office or voicemail at every break or trying to keep up-to-the-minute on emails, phone calls, etc. Such behaviors are costly: every time a person is distracted from a mental task (by a ringing phone, email notification, etc., or self-interrupts to check messages) it takes precious time to refocus and get back on track (see "Who Says So?"). Every time your direct reports are distracted during training, the class moves on and critical learning opportunities are missed.

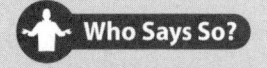 **Who Says So?**   *Interruptions Are Costly*

Much of the progress in the last thirty years has been the product of the creativity and intellectual capital of so-called "knowledge workers"—planners, designers, writers, programmers, scientists, managers, marketers, and so forth. Knowledge workers do their best and most productive work when they are in the "flow"—so fully concentrated on their work that they lose track of time and produce great output through absolute concentration (Csikszentmihalyi, 1990; Spolsky, 2000).

The trouble is that it is not easy to get into the "flow." It takes, on average, fifteen minutes for a knowledge worker to start working at maximum productivity. And it is all too easy to get knocked out of the flow. Any number of distractions—phone calls, instant messages, email alerts, questions from co-workers and on and on—are sufficient to throw a knowledge worker off. Taking just one minute to answer an email effectively costs sixteen minutes of high-productivity work.

Unnecessary interruptions are estimated to consume about 28 percent of the knowledge worker's day, which translates to 28 billion lost hours to companies in the United States alone (Spira & Feintuch, 2005).

The same applies to learning. Frequent and unnecessary interruptions—including self-generated interruptions ("I'll just quickly check my inbox")—disrupt the intense concentration needed to truly master a new topic or skill. A ringing cell phone alone reduces the amount learned (McDonald, Wiezorek, & Walter, 2004).

So, to maximize learning, shield your direct reports from as many interruptions as possible during the training and counsel them to focus their attention. People greatly overestimate their ability to "multi-task." While they are paying attention to one thing, they can completely miss another, even something as striking as a gorilla suddenly appearing on the scene (see the participant's guide, page 20).

"Businesses and schools praise multitasking," writes John Media, director of the Brain Center for Applied Learning Research, "but research clearly shows that it reduces productivity and increases mistakes" (Medina, 2008, p. 93).

Make Learning Assignments

The third aspect of your role in creating learning opportunities is for you to make specific work assignments that will require your direct report to put her or his newly acquired skills or knowledge to work.

So, for example, if the course was about project management, be sure your direct report has the opportunity to manage a project of appropriate size and complexity soon thereafter. If the program aimed to improve presentation skills, ask him or her to make an important presentation soon afterward. Timing is important; the more quickly new learning starts to be used, the better it can be recalled and put to use later. The longer the delay, the more will be forgotten.

Assignments that have an element of "stretch" in them are most effective. Use Worksheet 2.4 to help you think about opportunities for your direct report to use or practice new knowledge and skills.

WORKSHEET 2.4
Opportunities to Apply and Reinforce Learning

 **Do It Now**

Instructions

1. Use this form to help you identify ways to ensure that training and development are put to work.

2. In column 1, briefly summarize the objective(s) that you and your direct report agreed on.

3. In columns 2 and 3, brainstorm opportunities to apply newly acquired skills and knowledge—either within their current responsibilities or by taking on a special task or assignment.

4. Prioritize the opportunities and select ones that provide the best balance or personal development and departmental needs.

Direct Report's Objective (Briefly Restate)	Best Opportunities to Apply	
	Within Current Job Responsibilities	Special Assignments or Tasks
1.		
2.		
3.		

"You've been doing a great job, Wilson, and I think you deserve a treat"

Provide Feedback and Encouragement

The last and most critical way for you to be more engaged is by providing coaching—feedback, encouragement, and advice—in the post-training period.

When two people attend the same training program, the performance of the person whose manager actively provides coaching improves more and faster than the performance of the person whose manager is not actively engaged (see Who Says So? page 6).

> *People need feedback to become really good at anything.*

You make a difference. Superior performers in every field agree that coaches and coaching were vital for them to reach their full potential. No athlete ever made it to the Olympics, no performer to Carnegie Hall, without coaching. Business executives invariably credit mentors for helping them achieve success. Providing feedback and guidance for performance improvement are two of the most important jobs a manager has.

To be effective, the coaching needs to be:

- ☐ Frequent
- ☐ Balanced
- ☐ Specific
- ☐ A dialogue

Frequent

Most employees want more feedback on their performance than they currently receive. Managers consistently receive low marks on providing adequate feedback. The lack of feedback is understandable. At the pace of business today, it is easy to get so busy that you don't take the time to provide coaching and encouragement. But it is not forgivable; lack of feedback undermines employee commitment and is detrimental to performance.

If you find that you are too busy to remember to provide the feedback your employees need and want, then schedule "provide feedback" as a task on your calendar. It is at least as important as any other item on your agenda. Coaching is vital if you really want to get your money's worth from

"You call that high, Mr. Raskin?"

training and development. A few minutes invested in providing feedback and encouragement on a regular basis will pay continuing returns in the form of increased commitment and performance.

Balanced

According to Ken Blanchard, author of *The One-Minute Manager,* the only way that most employees know they have done a good job is when no one has yelled at them lately (Blanchard & Homan, 2004, p. x).

Make it a point to "catch people doing something right" and remark on it. In particular, recognize people who make the effort to try something new—"I really liked the way you made an effort to . . ."—even if the performance itself is not yet stellar. Employees want more feedback in general, but what they really crave is positive feedback—management's recognition of their efforts and accomplishments. Positive feedback is especially important if you want people to try new behaviors and approaches as part of a change initiative or following a training program.

To provide balanced coaching, you have to learn to give both positive as well as developmental or corrective feedback. It does not mean always giving them together in a "bad news sandwich." Stop sticking your "but" in everybody's feel-good moments: "I liked the way you . . . BUT. . . ."

If you don't do so already, practice giving positive feedback, period. Recognize a great effort, an improvement, etc., and then STOP. Give negative or corrective feedback privately and on a separate occasion.

Specific

While giving someone an "Attaboy" or "Attagirl" is better than providing no feedback at all, feedback and coaching need to be specific, as well as timely, to be optimally effective. Employees are quite adept at detecting and immune to the effects of insincere, sweeping platitudes: "Fine job, whoever you are, whatever it was."

The Center for Creative Leadership recommends providing feedback in a Situation-Behavior-Impact (SBI) format (Ting & Scisco, 2006):

- *Situation:* Describe a specific situation—a particular meeting, a specific report, client encounter, etc.

- Specify the *behavior*—say what you actually observed: "The way you handled the customer's objection," "How you organized your presentation," etc.
- Identify the *impact* on you and others: "Showed me that you really took the training seriously," "Made her feel valued and respected," "Convince me that you are ready for greater responsibility."

A Dialogue

Coaching at its best helps people solve their own problems, come to their own insights, and formulate their own plans. To achieve those ends, make your coaching a dialogue, rather than a lecture. Stimulate your direct reports' thinking, encourage them to draw on their own experiences, and prompt them to explore options. Spend more time asking than telling. Pay attention to who is doing the talking and who is coming up with observations and options; both you *and your direct report* should be contributing to the exploration of ideas and opportunities.

"Keep up the good work, whatever it is, whoever you are."

> *Effective coaching is a dialogue, not a lecture.*

Coaching and encouragement from you are so central to getting your money's worth from training and development that they deserved to be tracked like any other critical business activity. If your organization does not use online follow-through management, you can use Worksheet 2.5 to monitor your coaching performance. An important practice of "total quality management" is to prominently post performance charts; consider posting the worksheet in your office to help keep this vital activity top of mind.

If the program your direct report attends uses an electronic follow-through system, you will receive requests for feedback and coaching by email. Respond to these requests promptly to sustain your direct report's commitment and maximize the positive impact (see "Who Says So?"). Providing feedback through online systems will require only a few minutes of your time every couple of weeks, but it will create long-lived value for your direct reports, your department, and ultimately, you personally.

WORKSHEET 2.5
Coaching Scorecard

Do It Now

Instructions: For ten weeks after training, plot the number of interactions you have with your direct report related to the transfer and application of the learning program. Aim for two or more each week (even just a quick, "How are you doing on your learning goals?").

Number of Coaching Interactions

5+

4

3

2

1

0   1   2   3   4   5   6   7   8   9   10

Weeks Since Training

 *Prompt Feedback Fuels Efforts*

If you respond promptly to your direct report's request for feedback, she will be much more likely to sustain her efforts to improve.

The evidence comes from a study of over five thousand participants in a training program at a leading technology company (Wick, Pollock, Jefferson, & Flanagan, 2006, p. 154). The program used a follow-through management system called *Friday5s*® that encouraged participants to request feedback from their managers. The behavior of those who *received* a response to their request was dramatically different from those who requested feedback but received none. The group that received feedback was, on average, *twice* as likely to continue working and reporting on their goals.

This makes perfect sense from an employee's point of view. If you ask your manager for assistance with learning transfer and your manager provides it, it's a clear signal that he or she thinks what you are doing is important and worth your time. Conversely, if you ask for feedback and the request is ignored, it's an equally clear signal (intentional or unintentional) that your manger does not value your efforts to apply learning and that you should spend your time on other things.

So, if you want to get your money's worth from training, take the few minutes necessary to respond to each request for feedback.

Additional suggestions, more detailed descriptions, and examples are given in the GuideMe on Coaching.

 *Online Coaching Recommendations*

Online coaching can be a fast and efficient way to help your direct reports get their money's worth from training and development. It's a great option for geographically dispersed teams. If the training program uses a follow-through management system, you will receive email requests with links that allow you to view and comment on your direct reports' reports quickly and efficiently.

If your company has not yet implemented an automated follow-through system, ask your direct reports to periodically email you brief updates along the lines of Worksheet 2.7. Whichever system you use, tips for maximizing the efficiency and impact of online coaching include:

1. **Do it now.** That is, respond to the request as soon as you encounter it. Don't set it aside with the intention of getting back to it later—it is too easy to bury it under new messages and for you to forget to go back to it. It only takes a few minutes to respond; setting it aside and coming back to it later will actually take more time. A short, but prompt, response will likely have greater impact than a longer but delayed one.

2. **Scan the update.** Before you start to craft your response, quickly scan the whole update. Does anything catch your attention? Does it provide enough detail that you feel you know what is being done? What is your overall impression from your quick scan?

3. **Acknowledge the effort.** Regardless of your overall opinion of the progress report, start by positively acknowledging the effort and the request so that you encourage more of this behavior in the future. Use an opening along the lines of: "Thank you for continuing your efforts, submitting an update, and seeking feedback."

4. **Comment specifically.** While general accolades ("Keep up the good work!") are better than nothing, your feedback will have a much more beneficial impact if you comment on something specific in the report ("I especially like the way that you …" or "You seem to be struggling with…"). If your direct report asks a specific question, be certain to answer it.

5. **Ask a question or make a suggestion.** Use the coaching opportunity to stimulate your direct report's thinking and take him or her to a higher level of performance. If possible, ask a question ("Why do you think he reacted that way?" or "Have you ever considered …"). Or, if appropriate, make a suggestion— something to try, someone to talk to, an article to read, or something that has worked for you.

6. **Save your best responses.** Save any especially good responses you write in a separate document. That way, if the same issue comes up (and it is likely to when another of your direct reports attends the program), you will be able to retrieve the relevant comments, paste them in, and quickly personalize them in a fraction of the time that would be required for you to recreate and retype them.

3. Be More Results-Driven

You are pretty demanding when it comes to business results and quality. You hold yourself and your direct reports to high standards of performance—or you would not have been promoted to manager in the first place.

But even managers with a solid reputation for driving business performance often have a blind spot when it comes to getting results from training. They just don't treat developmental objectives with the same rigor, or give them the same kind of attention, as they do other business objectives. Such a double standard is counter-productive, since the only reason to invest in training and development is to improve business-relevant performance.

In the final analysis, development objectives *are* business objectives and they should be managed as such. You will increase the return you get from training and development by managing post-training execution with the same results focus you use to manage the execution of other business processes. Goals without execution are valueless.

> *"Without execution, the breakthrough thinking breaks down, learning adds no value, people don't meet their stretch goals, and the revolution stops dead in its tracks."*
>
> —Bossidy and Charan, 2002, p. 19

A results-driven approach to learning transfer and the execution of developmental goals includes:

☐ Endorsing objectives

☐ Monitoring progress

☐ Assessing results

☐ Planning further improvement

Endorsing Objectives

No competent manager would allow his or her direct reports to set their own business objectives without oversight or review. People might end up working on all sorts of initiatives that were only of minimal importance to the business, or they might select such easy-to-achieve targets that the organization would lose its competitive edge.

Yet that is precisely how most learning and development objectives are managed. Employees go off to a training or development program, set their own goals, put them in their notebooks, and promptly forget about them. You have probably done it yourself. Managers rarely review, much less rigorously follow up on training and development goals. No wonder training often produces minimal impact.

In a not atypical case study, only 40 percent of managers had any idea what their direct reports were working on after a week-long, $2,500 program (Wick, Pollock, Jefferson, & Flanagan, 2006, p. 128). How many of the 60 percent of participants whose managers had no clue what their goals were do you think took the responsibility to use their learning seriously? What company would achieve its business plan if 60 percent of the managers did not know the objectives of their direct reports?

Compare your knowledge of your own reports' business goals versus their developmental goals. You must fix this weak link in the value chain if you are to improve the return on your learning investment.

Review and endorse or revise your direct report's goals for learning transfer, just as you would for his or her other objectives. Make sure the goals complement your direct report's existing business objectives and that they reflect the best opportunities you agreed would improve performance.

If the program employs a follow-through management system, then your direct report's goals will be sent to you automatically a week after the program. Take a few minutes to review the goals for criticality, focus, and clarity and respond using the built-in feedback form. Worksheet 2.6 will save you time and simplify the process. If your company does not yet employ an online system, ask your direct reports to send you copies of their goals and review them using the checklist criteria.

WORKSHEET 2.6
Evaluating Goals

Do It Now

Instructions: Below are the key criteria for evaluating learning transfer goals. Suggested responses are provided depending on whether the goal does, or does not, meet the criterion. Responses can be strung together with appropriate conjunctions to create a comprehensive response (e.g., "Your goal is well written and clear, but I do not think you have chosen one of the best opportunities …").

☑	Criterion	Suggested Feedback	
		Meets Criterion	**Does Not Meet**
☐	**Clarity** It is immediately clear what the person hopes to accomplish	"Your goal is well written and clear."	"You need to rewrite your goal; I am still unclear exactly what it is you hope to accomplish. Please be more specific."
☐	**Importance** The objective focuses on an important aspect of performance for this individual and program.	"You have selected a key opportunity to apply what you have learned to improve your performance."	"I do not think you have chosen one of the best opportunities to improve your performance. I'd rather see you focus on…."
☐	**Timeline** The time to achieve this goal or milestone is specified	The time line is defined.	"You neglected to define when you expect to achieve this objective. Please add the due date to your goal."
☐	**Relevance** The proposed goal is directly relevant to the person's current business objectives or is vital to prepare him/her for the next level of responsibility.	"I am pleased to see that you have selected a goal related to your existing objectives so that you can use your ongoing work as your 'practice field.'" or "I am pleased to see that your goal is to develop skills that you will need to prepare you for greater responsibilities."	"I do not see the connection between this goal and your existing priorities. That will make it harder to accomplish. Can you tie it to something that is already 'on your plate'?" or "I think you should focus on building skills that you will need to prepare you for greater responsibility."
☐	**Measures of Success** The goal includes a description of how progress and achievement will be evident or assessed.	"You have clearly defined the indicators of success for this goal, which is essential. You have to keep score if you want to get better."	"You have not defined how you will assess progress or achievement. What are the measures of success? How will you (and I) know?"
☐	**Stretch** The objective requires some stretch—a significant improvement in performance—not just something the person does already.	"I am pleased that you have given yourself a challenging 'stretch' goal. We need to set targets for ourselves that are beyond our current capabilities if we are to continue to grow and improve."	"I am disappointed that you have defined a goal with very little challenge to it—something you can achieve with very little effort. I'd like to see you set a more challenging target."
☐	**Realistic** The targeted level of achievement is appropriate for the time and resources available.	"This looks achievable if you work at it diligently. Let me know if you need assistance or run into unexpected difficulties."	"I admire your enthusiasm, but I am concerned that you have set the target unrealistically high given the time available. Please revisit the target and/or the timeline. You may want to define the key milestone that you will achieve within this time."

Monitoring Progress

Good managers pay attention to key indicators of progress in their areas of responsibility, such as project milestones, financial results, customer service ratings, and so forth. Indeed, "to manage" means to monitor, assess, and adjust as necessary to ensure that the organization achieves its objectives.

Similarly, the execution of learning and development plans also must be actively managed if the organization is to get its money's worth from training. There are well-defined reporting periods for business results. Projects have defined milestones. Regularly scheduled updates should likewise be defined for learning and development goals.

A reporting schedule will, itself, help your direct reports keep their follow-through objectives top of mind. Periodic updates will allow you to monitor progress, recognize effort, and take corrective action if the expected improvement is not being achieved—in short, to manage the process.

Periodic updates also improve outcomes as a result of the "spacing effect" in learning. Fifty years of learning research has shown that sustainability is improved when learners have to revisit new knowledge periodically. (See "Who Says So?")

 **Who Says So?**   *Spacing Is Important*

The best way to get learning to "stick"—to be sustained so that it can be recalled and used later—is to revisit the topic several times at intervals (Medina, 2009, p. 100). Based on an extensive review of the learning research, Thalheimer (2006) concluded that "Spacing learning over time produces substantial learning benefits" and "real learning doesn't usually occur in one-time events."

Spacing is particularly beneficial when long-term retention is the goal, as in most training initiatives. Managers can take advantage of the spacing effect by requiring periodic updates on the progress being made to put the new learning to work. Each time an update is due, the learner has to retrieve and revisit what he or she learned, which reinforces the memory trace and helps minimize forgetting.

Requiring repeated *retrieval* of learning at intervals produces greater benefits than merely repeating the presentation of the material. This is especially true when retrieval practice is accompanied by feedback (Thalheimer, 2006). Longer intervals tend to stimulate longer retention, so space updates two to four weeks apart.

If the program your direct report attends uses an automated follow-through system, then a reporting schedule will have already been established; your direct report can simply send you copies of his or her updates as appropriate. If the course itself does not include a robust follow-through process, you should establish your own. Updates can be brief (a paragraph or two per objective). *Having* and *sticking to* a schedule for monitoring progress is more important than the specific content or format of the updates. Use or adapt Worksheet 2.7 if you do not already have a reporting format.

WORKSHEET 2.7
Update Schedule and Form

Do It Now

Participant: _____   Manager: _____

Updates Scheduled for (fill in dates):

☐ 1: _____   ☐ 2: _____   ☐ 3: _____
☐ 4: _____   ☐ 5: _____

On each date above, copy and complete this form and send to manager.

Goal 1 (briefly stated):

Actions taken in this reporting period and results (if any):

Progress: ☐ None ☐ Some ☐ Significant ☐ Goal achieved
   Plan for coming weeks:

Goal 2 (briefly stated):

Actions taken in this reporting period:

Progress: ☐ None ☐ Some ☐ Significant ☐ Goal achieved
   Plan for coming weeks:

Additional comments, questions, or requests for assistance:

Require updates on learning objectives every two to four weeks for three to six months. (See FAQ: Isn't This a Lot of Busy Work?) Adjust the schedule as necessary for different kinds of training and goals. For example, changing interpersonal skills takes longer sustained practice than mastering a specific technical or sales technique. Continue the reporting process long and frequently enough for the new behaviors to become habit. Stop, or define new objectives, before the reports become a meaningless ritual.

 ## Isn't This Just a Lot of Busy Work?

You may be thinking, "Look, we are all adults here and we've got a business to run. This requiring updates on learning objectives seems like a lot of HR busy work."

Requiring periodic reports on progress toward development goals is busy work if either of two conditions apply:

- Your company considers financial reporting, project team milestones, and strategic initiative updates to be just "busy work."
- The reports are treated as busy work.

It is very unlikely that the first condition holds. No organization bigger than a mom-and-pop shop can achieve its business goals without some sort of reporting system and schedule. While managers may not enjoy preparing monthly or quarterly reports, they understand that the requirement to periodically assess and report business results is essential to ensure that initiatives are on track and that financial and other business objectives are being met.

Why should reporting on personal development goals be any different than reporting on business development goals? Both represent investments that are important to the future of the company. Organizations invest in training and development to improve future performance. As such, development objectives are business objectives and should be managed similarly.

Even so, reporting progress on development goals will be just "busy work" if you, as manager, treat it as such. That is, you determine whether such reports drive improvement or are a waste of time—the same as with any other business report. If you take them seriously—read and comment on them—so will your direct reports, and their updates will be prepared with thought and care. If you ignore their reports or treat them superficially, then their execution and preparation will be superficial, perfunctory and of low value.

The requirement to periodically report and explain financial results keeps managers focused and striving to achieve their targets. Meaningful reporting and discussion of developmental goals will have the same effect. It's not busy work if you want your money's worth.

If you already require regular updates from your direct reports on their business objectives, simply have them include their developmental objectives as part of those updates. For this to be effective, however, you must give the developmental objectives the same scrutiny, recognition, and commentary that you give their other objectives.

Assessing Results

Every race has a finish line; every fiscal period has a closing date. While the quest for performance improvement should never stop, each cycle should have an end-point at which progress is assessed and appropriate recognition is given.

Contrary to popular belief, the last day of class is not the finish line for training and development.

> *The real work begins when the coursework ends.*

Participants have not truly completed the program until they have incorporated what was taught into their day-to-day work. The "final examination" for corporate training is on-the-job, improved performance.

More enlightened companies now wait to award certificates, issue credit for completing the program, or provide other recognition until there is evidence of ongoing use and improvement. As manager, it is up to you define the finish line and what constitutes successful completion . . . just as you do for business objectives.

Meet with your direct report soon after the training course to define when the "final examination" will be and how success will be defined. Set a firm date for a wrap-up meeting at which time you will expect your direct report to:

- Assess changes in her or his capabilities;
- Give specific examples of the results that were achieved; and
- Reflect on the development experience itself—what helped, what hurt, what could make the process even more effective in the future?

Recommendations for conducting the wrap-up discussion meeting are given in the GuideMe below.

 **GuideMe®** *Recommendations for Wrap-Up Meeting*

Overview

1. The reasons to have a final meeting for each round of development are to underscore your expectation for improvement, to assess what progress has been made, to recognize achievement, and to plan for future development.

2. Schedule the "final exam" meeting as part of the overall follow-through to training.

3. Set the date two to six months after the program, so that improvement (if any) will be evident.

4. Plan for approximately a thirty-minute discussion. As with the pre-training meeting, the meeting's length is less important than that it scheduled and conducted.

The five key questions to ask are:

• What new or enhanced capabilities have you developed?

• What did you accomplish as a result (and what is the evidence)?

• What helped the most in (or prevented you from) achieving your goals?

• What advice do you have for others attending this program?

• What do you think you need to do next to continue your development?

Detailed Coaching Guide

1. Meet and greet. Thank the person for meeting with you. Express your interest in hearing about what he or she has been able to achieve.

2. Ask: "Comparing your performance now to your performance before training, do you feel you have any new or enhanced capability as a result of the training and follow-through?"

   • Listen carefully to the answer.

   • Play it back to be sure you understood: "So, you feel you are now better able to . . . ."

   • If you concur, reinforce the conclusion. If you disagree, ask for examples (see below).

3. Ask: "What were you able to accomplish?"

   • Listen carefully to the answer.

   • Play it back to be sure you understood: "So, you feel the most important thing you accomplished was. . . ."

   • Ask for specific examples to ensure that there is evidence to back the claims. Encourage your direct report to "tell the story."

4. Ask: "What helped the most?" (if he or she has good examples) or "What got in the way of making greater progress?" (if he or she has weak or no evidence)

   • Encourage reflection so you both learn how to get even greater improvement in the future.

   • If progress was not great, ask the person to rate his or her own effort. Did he/she give it the best effort?

   • If he or she blames the course, reflect on what he or she said about it immediately afterward—is it different? If the person has legitimate criticism about the utility or applicability, relay the information to the program sponsor so he/she can take corrective action.

5. Ask: "What advice do you have for others attending this program?"
   - The goal is to encourage critical thinking. You will also gain information that will help you help future attendees.
6. Ask: "What do you think you need to do next to continue your development?"
   - Self-development and improvement should be a never-ending activity.
   - The purpose is to get the person thinking about what he or she must do next and to allow you to point the person in the right direction.
   - Ask the person to think about the personal and business benefits to be sure he or she has picked the most valuable areas for focus.
7. Summarize the key points and action plans.

If substantial improvement or results have been achieve, recognize and praise the person. If little or no improvement was achieved, express your disappointment. Ask what got in the way. Try to understand why no improvement was achieved so that you can prevent a reoccurrence.

If it appears it really was the training that was inadequate or misdirected (as opposed to a lack of follow-through), then you need to let the training department and its management know so that the problem can be addressed. If the problem was lack of effort or follow-through on the part of your direct report, voice your concern about continuing to invest in this person's development.

If the problem was that you did not have (read, "did not make") the time to provide coaching and support, then you know what the solution is.

"So, Jim, where do you see yourself in ten minutes?"

Planning Further Improvement

The last agenda item for the closing discussion should be to plan the next cycle of development. Personal development should be an ongoing effort. Set the expectation for continuous improvement—that your direct report will sustain and then extend the progress made to date.

In the participant's guide, we recommend that your direct reports come prepared to discuss the most important thing to do next to continue their development and further their careers (see page 46 of the participant's guide). You should ponder the same question so you can review and discuss their plans. Taking a few moments to complete Worksheet 2.8 will help.

WORKSHEET 2.8
Future Development Plans

Do It Now

Participant: _____   Manager: _____

Instructions

1. In column 1, list the three next best opportunities for your direct report to improve his or her performance and value to the organization. Start with a verb like "increase," "start," "stop," "improve," etc. In some cases, the most important thing to do will be to sustain or more fully develop recently acquired capabilities.

2. In column 2, list some potential developmental activities relevant to the specific need. Think broadly (beyond just training programs) to include on-the-job learning, special assignments, mentoring, self-study, etc. Don't feel you have to have all the answers. Ask human resources or, better yet, task your direct report to explore opportunities.

Top Developmental Opportunities	Possible Developmental Activities
1.	
2.	
3.	

Close the loop. The last step after your "final exam" meeting is to close the loop by summarizing, in writing, the outcome. This is critical for two reasons:

1. To reward and encourage those who took the application of training seriously and improved their performance as a result.

2. To prove that you are serious about putting training to work by drawing attention to those who fail to do so. The grapevine in most companies is such that you will only have to write one or two "dunning" letters before people get the message.

Your summary will also be a helpful reference for performance reviews. A template to help you get started is provided in Worksheet 2.9.

Summary and Closing Thoughts

Effective training and development programs are essential for companies to retain their human capital and remain competitive in a rapidly changing and challenging market.

As a manager, you have a profound influence on the effectiveness of training. When it produces improved performance, you deserve much of the credit. If the time and money are wasted, you bear much of the responsibility.

Getting your money's worth from training and development requires co-investing some of your time to leverage your employees' efforts and the company's resources. You will earn a return on your investment of time through improved performance, greater commitment, and enhanced capabilities of those who report to you. You will also improve your own chances for advancement by earning a reputation as a developer of people and builder of strong teams.

Our goal in writing this guide was to help managers get their money's worth from training efficiently, effectively, and well, so that everyone benefits. We look forward to learning about your successes and your ideas on how to make this guide even more helpful to managers and participants in the future.

WORKSHEET 2.9
Summary of Overall Evaluation

 **Do It Now**

Instructions: Close the loop by using the template below to summarize, in writing, the overall outcome of the training and development initiative. To get your money's worth, positively recognize those who made significant progress and redirect those who failed to take full advantage of the opportunity.

FOR SOMEONE WHO MADE SIGNIFICANT IMPROVEMENT

Dear _____,

Thank you for meeting with me to discuss the progress you have made in applying the principles of the _____ program. Overall, I am very pleased with the progress you have made, especially in the areas of _____ and _____. I want to commend you particularly on the way that you worked diligently toward your goals and applied what you learned. You have demonstrated the ability to continue to grow and learn, something that will serve you well throughout your career.

In the spirit of continuous improvement, we agreed that the next best development opportunities for you are to _____ and _____ by _____.

Congratulations again on the fine progress you have made.

Sincerely,

_____

FOR SOMEONE WHO FAILED TO IMPROVE

Dear _____,

Thank you for meeting with me to discuss the progress you have made in applying the principles of the _____ program. As we discussed, I am disappointed that you were not able to give specific examples of how you had improved your performance by applying what you learned. Others who attended the same program did.

I realize that you encountered some obstacles, including _____ and _____ _____. Nevertheless, demonstrating the ability to learn and grow even in the face of business challenges is important to your long-term career.

If you are given the opportunity to participate in another learning and development program in the future, I expect you to devote greater time and effort to implementing what you learn, so that both you and the company get a better return on the investment.

Sincerely,

_____

References and Recommended Reading for Managers

American Express. (2007). The real ROI of leadership development: Comparing classroom vs. online vs. blended delivery. www.ninthhouse.com/philosophy/library.asp. Accessed September 2008.

Blanchard, S., & Homan, M. (2004). *Leverage your best, ditch the rest: The coaching secrets top executives depend on.* New York: HarperCollins.

Bossidy, L., & Charan, R. (2002). *Execution: The discipline of getting things done.* New York: Crown Business.

Brinkerhoff, R.O., & Apking, A.M. (2001). *High impact learning: Strategies for leveraging business results from training.* New York: Basic Books.

Broad, M.L., & Newstrom, J.W. (1992). *Transfer of training: Action-packed strategies to ensure high payoff from training investments.* Cambridge, MA: Perseus.

Burton, R.J., & McDonald-Mann, D. (1999) *Giving feedback to subordinates.* Greensboro, NC: Center for Creative Leadership.

Clemmer, J. (2009). Why most training fails. www.clemmer.net/articles/Why_Most_Training_Fails_Skill_Development.aspx. Accessed September 2008.

Colvin, G. (2006, October). What it takes to be great. *Fortune,* pp. 88–96.

Csikszentmihalyi, M. (1990). *Flow: The psychology of optimal experience.* New York: Harper & Row.

Echols, M.E. (2008). *Creating value with human capital investment.* Wyomissing, PA: Tapestry Press.

Ericsson, K.A., Prietula, M.J., & Cokely, E.T. (2007, July/August). The making of an expert. *Harvard Business Review,* pp. 115–121.

Foxon, M. (1993). A process approach to the transfer of training. Part 1: The impact of motivation and supervisor support on transfer maintenance. *Australian Journal of Educational Technology, 9*(2), 130–143. www.ascilite.org.au/ajet/ajet9/foxon.html. Accessed September 2008.

Kouzes, J., & Posner, B. (2007). *The leadership challenge* (4th ed.). San Francisco: Jossey-Bass.

McDonald, D.D., Wiczorek, M., & Walker, C. (2004). Factors affecting learning during health education sessions. *Clinical Nursing Research, 13*(2), 156–167.

Medina, J.J. (2008). *Brain rules: 12 principles for surviving and thriving at work, home and school.* Seattle, WA: Pear Press.

Ross, P.E. (2006, August). The expert mind. *Scientific American,* pp. 64–71.

Stewart, M. (2007, November). Best of the best. *Learning Alert,* 26. www.ifollow through.com/news/learning_alert/learningalert26.html. Accessed September 2008.

Spira, J.B., & Feintuch, J.B. (2005). *The cost of not paying attention: How interruptions impact knowledge worker productivity.* New York: Basex.

Spolsky, J. (2000). Where do these people get their (unoriginal) ideas? www.joelon software.com/articles/fog0000000068.html. Accessed September 2008.

Thalheimer, W. (2006, February). *Spacing learning events over time: What the research says.* Retrieved June 2008 from www.work-learning.com/catalog/

Ting, S., & Scisco, P. (2006). *The CCL handbook of coaching: A guide for the leader coach.* San Francisco: Jossey-Bass.

Wick, C.W., Pollock, R.V.H., Jefferson, A. McK., & Flanagan, R.D. (2006). *The six disciplines of breakthrough learning: How to turn training and development into business results.* San Francisco: Pfeiffer.

Wick, C.W., Jefferson, A. McK., & Pollock, R.V.H. (2008). Learning transfer: The next frontier. In E. Biech (Ed), *ASTD handbook for workplace learning professionals.* Alexandria, VA: ASTD Press.

Wiggenhorn, W. (1990, July/August). Motorola U: When training becomes education. *Harvard Business Review,* p. 75.

Appendix

Completed Examples for Managers*

COMPLETED EXAMPLE OF WORKSHEET 2.1
Opportunities for Improvement

 **Do It Now**

Instructions: List three things that your direct report could do faster, better, or more effectively that would make him or her even more valuable to your organization:

1. Accentuate the positive. Be careful about not always complaining. You are getting a reputation as a "whiner" and people are beginning to discount what you say.

2. Slow down and listen to your customers. Probe for their real needs. Be sure you understand the problem before you propose the solution.

3. Continue to refine your presentation skills. This is an area of strength for you; be sure to build on it.

---

*Additional examples are available on the book's website, www.pfeiffer.com/go/forthill
Once on the website, use the password **reference** to access the files.

COMPLETED EXAMPLES OF WORKSHEET 2.2
WIIFM for Managers

 Do It Now

Your Name: *Chris Cashman*

Name of Program: *Hope Is Not a Strategy*

Date of Program: *August 13–15, 2009*

Instructions for Managers

1. In the first column, write two to five bullet points that summarize the key deliverables for your unit. Why does your group exist? How does your group create value for the business? This step is important: training and development must ultimately support the organization's objectives.

2. In column 2, write out the specific results for which your direct report is personally responsible. Ideally, these should mesh with her/his annual performance goals.

3. Refer to Worksheet 2.1: No matter how good your direct report is, he or she can get better at something, either to do the current job better or to prepare for greater responsibility. What do the top performers, the best of the best, in the field do better than your direct report can do currently? List the best opportunities for improvement in this column.

4. Look at the course description and objectives. What does it cover that is relevant to this employee? What does it promise? [If you don't know, find out.]

5. Put columns 3 and 4 together to fill in column 5. What do you want your direct report to do better and differently as a result of attending the program that will improve his or her personal performance and that of your department?

6. Review your completed WIIFM Worksheet with your direct report. He or she should have completed one independently (Worksheet 1.2). Compare notes and perceptions.

7. Agree on the top learning objectives for the forthcoming program.

	1. Most important deliverables of our business/ organizational unit	2. Most important results for which this person is responsible	3. What new or improved skills/ knowledge would help him/her deliver better results	4. Relevant topics covered in the training or development program	5. What I want him/her to do better or differently afterward to improve performance
Your Input	– revenue growth – sustained profitability	– sales to new and existing customers	– better sales planning and territory management – improved customer segmentation and marketing	– developing sales plans – selling to teams and multiple buyers – identifying most valuable prospects	– increase yield by targeting and closing higher-value customers – make better use of time

COMPLETED EXAMPLE OF WORKSHEET 2.3
Learning Memorandum

 **Do It Now**

Instructions: Complete and send this memorandum only if you have not received one from your direct report and the training is mandatory.

Dear Pat,

Thank you for meeting with me the other day to discuss the upcoming Effective Project Management program. I am disappointed that I have not received your summary of that discussion that I asked you to prepare. I hope this is not indicative of the effort you will put into preparing and following up on your education. Since you did not summarize the meeting as I asked, I have below:

We agreed that the most important thing for you to focus on during the course was running effective meetings in order to improve your performance in the areas of time management (for you and others), RACI analysis, agreed-upon action items, and improved follow-through.

You agreed to do all the assignments, give the program your full attention, and practice your new skills / knowledge afterward. We scheduled a post-course follow up meeting on July 15th at 8:30 a.m., at which I will ask you to share your reaction to the program, your most important insights, and your specific goals for improving your performance.

Sincerely,

Stephane

COMPLETED EXAMPLE OF WORKSHEET 2.4
Opportunities to Apply and Reinforce Learning

 **Do It Now**

Instructions

1. Use this form to help you identify ways to ensure that training and development are put to work.

2. In column 1, briefly summarize the objective(s) that you and your direct report agreed on.

3. In columns 2 and 3, brainstorm opportunities to apply newly acquired skills and knowledge—either within their current responsibilities or by taking on a special task or assignment.

4. Prioritize the opportunities and select ones that provide the best balance or personal development and departmental needs.

Direct Report's Objective (Briefly Restate)	Best Opportunities to Apply	
	Within Current Job Responsibilities	Special Assignments or Tasks
Improve active listening skills to improve teamwork	Primarily an on-the-job activity Ask for feedforward to help raise awareness of the goal and get ideas for action	Read "Into Action Guide" on active listening Complete online module on identifying non-verbal communication
Deepen understanding of marketing principles and apply to department's value proposition		Read "Positioning" Lead cross-functional team on defining and communicating our value statement. Attend Marketing's monthly "after action" reviews

COMPLETED EXAMPLE OF WORKSHEET 2.5
Coaching Scorecard

Do It Now

Instructions: For ten weeks after training, plot the number of interactions you have with your direct report related to the transfer and application of the learning program. Aim for two or more each week (even just a quick, "How are you doing on your learning goals?").

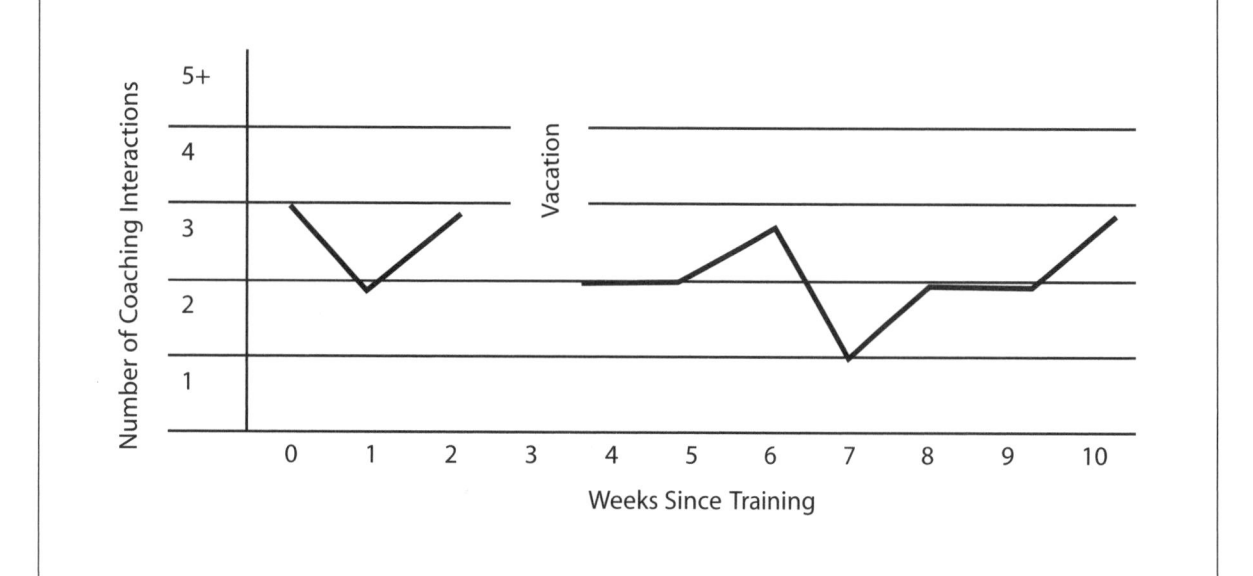

COMPLETED EXAMPLE OF WORKSHEET 2.6
Evaluating Goals

Instructions: Below are the key criteria for evaluating learning transfer goals. Suggested responses are provided depending on whether the goal does, or does not, meet the criterion. Responses can be strung together with appropriate conjunctions (e.g., "Your goal is well written and clear, but I do not think you have chosen one of the best opportunities . . . .")

☑	Criterion	Suggested Feedback	
		Meets Criterion	**Does Not Meet**
☑	**Clarity** It is immediately clear what the person hopes to accomplish	"Your goal is well written and clear."	"You need to rewrite your goal; I am still unclear exactly what it is you hope to accomplish. Please be more specific."
☑	**Importance** The objective focuses on an important aspect of performance for this individual and program.	"You have selected a key opportunity to apply what you have learned to improve your performance."	"I do not think you have chosen one of the best opportunities to improve your performance. I'd rather see you focus on. . . ."
☑	**Timeline** The time to achieve this goal or milestone is specified	The time line is defined.	"You neglected to define when you expect to achieve this objective. Please add the due date to your goal."
☐	**Relevance** The proposed goal is directly relevant to the person's current business objectives or is vital to prepare him/her for the next level of responsibility.	"I am pleased to see that you have selected a goal related to your existing objectives so that you can use your ongoing work as your 'practice field.'" or "I am pleased to see that your goal is to develop skills that you will need to prepare you for greater responsibilities."	"I do not see the connection between this goal and your existing priorities. That will make it harder to accomplish. Can you tie it to something that is already on your plate?" or "I think you should focus on building skills that you will need to prepare you for greater responsibility."
☑	**Measures of Success** The goal includes a description of how progress and achievement will be evident or assessed.	"You have clearly defined the indicators of success for this goal, which is essential. You have to keep score if you want to get better."	"You have not defined how you will assess progress or achievement. What are the measures of success? How will you (and I) know?"
☑	**Stretch** The objective requires some stretch—a significant improvement in performance—not just something the person does already.	"I am pleased that you have given yourself a challenging 'stretch' goal. We need to set targets for ourselves that are beyond our current capabilities if we are to continue to grow and improve."	"I am disappointed that you have defined a goal with very little challenge to it—something you can achieve with very little effort. I'd like to see you set a more challenging target."
☑	**Realistic** The targeted level of achievement is appropriate for the time and resources available.	"This looks achievable if you work at it diligently. Let me know if you need assistance or run into unexpected difficulties."	"I admire your enthusiasm, but I am concerned that you have set the target unrealistically high given the time available. Please revisit the targets and/or the timeline. You may want to define the key milestone that you will achieve within this time."

Feedback That Was Sent

Dear Bruce,

I have reviewed your goal from the Excellence in Execution program. Your goal is well written and clear and the time line is defined. You have selected a key opportunity to apply what you have learned to improve your performance, although I do not see the connection between this goal and your existing priorities. That will make it harder to accomplish. Can you tie it to something that is already "on your plate"?

You have clearly defined the indicators of success for this goal, which is essential. You have to keep score if you want to get better.

I am pleased that you have given yourself a challenge "stretch" goal. We need to set targets for ourselves beyond our current capabilities so that we continue to grow and improve. This looks achievable if you work at it diligently. Let me know if you need assistance or run into unexpected difficulties.

Best regards,
Agneta

COMPLETED EXAMPLE OF WORKSHEET 2.7
Update Schedule and Form

Do It Now

Participant: ____Un Yee Ling____   Manager: ____Carlos Manque____

Updates Scheduled for (fill in dates):

☑ 1: _October 10_   ☐ 2: _October 24_   ☐ 3: _November 7_
☐ 4: _November 21_   ☐ 5: _December 5_

On each date above, copy and complete this form and send to manager.

Goal 1 (briefly stated): Improve efficiency by improving time management skills.

Actions taken in this reporting period and results (if any):

Met with my team and thanked them for the feedback. Shared my goals for improvement and asked for ideas on how I could best achieve them.

Progress: ☐ None ☑ Some ☐ Significant ☐ Goal achieved

   Plan for coming weeks:

Do not check my email in the morning until I have first reviewed and prioritized my task list so I do not get suckered into dealing with "urgent" but unimportant issues.

Goal 2 (briefly stated): Spend more time on my high-potential prospects

Actions taken in this reporting period:

Went through my list of current prospects and ranked them from highest to lowest in terms of overall potential. Then looked at where I was spending my time. Found several significant mismatches, which I intend to fix in the coming weeks.

Progress: ☐ None ☑ Some ☐ Significant ☐ Goal achieved

   Plan for coming weeks:

Keep a log of where I am spending my time and check it against my prioritized list. Also, research several of the prospects where I did not really have enough data/insight to prioritize them. Adjust ranking as necessary.

Additional comments, questions, or requests for assistance: I would like to review my assessments of my direct reports and ideas for their continued development with you.

COMPLETED EXAMPLE OF WORKSHEET 2.8
Future Development Plans

Do It Now

Participant: _____Clay Coyle_____   Manager: _____Marcel Moreau_____

Instructions

1. In column 1, list the three next best opportunities for your direct report to improve his or her performance and value to the organization. Start with a verb like "increase," "start," "stop," "improve," etc. In some cases, the most important thing to do will be to sustain or more fully develop recently acquired capabilities.

2. In column 2, list some potential developmental activities relevant to the specific need. Think broadly (beyond just training programs) to include on-the-job learning, special assignments, mentoring, self-study, etc. Don't feel you have to have all the answers. Ask human resources or, better yet, task your direct report to explore opportunities.

Top Developmental Opportunities	Possible Developmental Opportunities
1. Become more knowledgeable about the principles of strategic marketing and apply them to your own work to improve its impact.	• Course in strategic marketing • Sit in on marketing reviews • Rotational assignment in marketing • Readings and follow-up discussions • Mentoring by RP who is very good in this regard
2. Learn to better organize your proposals and presentations so that they flow logically and anticipate questions and objections in order to increase their acceptance rate.	• Observing presentations and learning to critique them; discussing with me • Read "Structure of Arguments"
3.	

COMPLETED EXAMPLE OF WORKSHEET 2.9
Summary of Overall Evaluation

Instructions: Close the loop by using the template below to summarize, in writing, the overall outcome of the training and development initiative. To get your money's worth, positively recognize those who made significant progress and redirect those who failed to take full advantage of the opportunity.

FOR SOMEONE WHO MADE SIGNIFICANT IMPROVEMENT

Dear <u>Alex,</u>

Thank you for meeting with me to discuss the progress you have made in applying the principles of the <u>Finance for Non-Financial Managers</u> program. Overall, I am very pleased with the progress you have made, especially in the areas of <u>taking cash flow into consideration when evaluating marketing programs</u> and <u>applying pricing strategy</u>. I want to commend you particularly on the way that you worked diligently toward your goals to apply what you learned. You have demonstrated the ability to continue to grow and learn, something that will serve you well throughout your career.

In the spirit of continuous improvement, we agreed that the next best development opportunities for you are to <u>learn how to help your team develop a shared vision</u> and <u>developing at least one potential successor to your position</u> by <u>reading The Leadership Challenge and discussing it with me</u> and by <u>attending an appropriate leadership development program in six to nine months.</u>

Congratulations again on the fine progress you have made.

Sincerely,

<u>Marie</u>

FOR SOMEONE WHO FAILED TO IMPROVE

Dear <u>Lucinda,</u>

Thank you for meeting with me to discuss the progress you have made in applying the principles of the <u>Front Line Supervisor</u> Program. As we discussed, I am disappointed that you were not able to give specific examples of how you had improved your performance by applying what you learned. Others who attended the same program did.

I realize that you encountered some obstacles, including <u>being short-staffed</u> and <u>my heavy travel schedule.</u> Nevertheless, demonstrating the ability to learn and grow even in the face of business challenges is important to your long-term career.

If you are given the opportunity to participate in another learning and development program in the future, I expect you to devote greater time and effort to implementing what you learn, so that both you and the company get a better return on the investment.

Sincerely,

<u>Andy</u>

About the Authors

Andrew McK. Jefferson, JD, is president and chief executive officer for the Fort Hill Company. He excels in helping companies maximize the value they realize from their investments in learning and development. Andy is an accomplished executive with deep line management expertise. He understands the challenges of running a company and the importance of making every investment count. Prior to joining Fort Hill, he served as the chief executive officer of Vital Home Services and chief operating officer and general counsel of AmeriStar Technologies, Inc. He spent the early years of his career as an attorney focused on corporate and complex transactions.

Andy is a graduate of the University of Delaware and graduated with honors from the Widener University School of Law, where he currently serves on the school's Board of Overseers.

Roy V.H. Pollock, DVM, Ph.D., is the chief learning officer of the Fort Hill Company. A popular speaker who loves to teach and learn, he has a passion for helping individuals and teams succeed. Roy brings a broad range of business and educational acumen to his consulting. Prior to joining Fort Hill, Roy served as vice president, global strategic product development for SmithKline Beecham Animal Health; vice president, Companion Animal Division for Pfizer; president of IDEXX Informatics; and president of VetConnect Systems, Inc.

Roy has a longstanding interest in education and leadership development and is a Fellow of the Kellogg Foundation National Leadership Program. A graduate of Williams College, he earned his D.V.M. and Ph.D. degrees from Cornell University, where he was a member of the faculty for eight years, including four as assistant dean for curriculum. He has received

numerous awards, including the Ralston-Purina Research Award and the American Animal Hospital Association's Veterinarian of the Year.

Calhoun W. Wick is the chairman and founder of the Fort Hill Company. He is nationally recognized for his work on improving the performance of leaders and organizations. Cal was named "Thought Leader of the Year" by ISA, the Association of Learning Providers, in 2006. In 2007, Cal received the first-ever Neon Elephant Award from Work-Learning Research, Inc., "awarded to a person, team, or organization exemplifying enlightenment, integrity, and innovation in the field of workplace learning and performance."

Cal earned his master's degree as an Alfred P. Sloan Fellow at MIT's Sloan School of Management. His goal is nothing less than to transform the training and development industry.

About Fort Hill

Fort Hill is a consulting, training, and learning technology company that focuses exclusively on helping organizations and individuals put learning to work and prove and improve its impact. We are committed to the proposition that learning creates competitive advantage for individuals and organizations, provided it is properly targeted, supported, and applied.

In today's competitive market, no one can afford to waste time or money. Training and development programs need to pay a return in terms of improved individual and business performance. They can no longer be a series of isolated events that are attended and checked off a list. Real learning is an end-to-end process that delivers results.

In our research, we identified six factors that characterize high-impact programs (Wick, Pollock, Jefferson, & Flanagan, 2006). Recognizing that transfer and application were the weakest links in turning learning into results, Fort Hill originated the concept of Follow-Through Management®. We developed a suite of web-based Follow-Through Tools® that have been used by more than 85,000 participants in over forty-eight countries.

We also provide advice and consultation on best practices of program design, execution, measurement, follow-through, and marketing to help organizations enhance the beneficial impact of their learning and development efforts.

The research is clear: For learning and development to pay a dividend, participants and their managers need to co-invest in the process. They must work together to ensure that learning takes place and gets used.

Our clients asked us to develop a practical guide to facilitate this partnership. The workbook you are holding is the result.

Getting Your Money's Worth
······ for Managers ······

1
Be More Upfront

- Do your homework
- Meet before training
- Make expectations clear
- Schedule follow-up

3
Be More Results Driven

- Endorse objectives
- Monitor progress
- Assess results
- Plan further improvement

2
Be More Engaged

- Just ask
- Create opportunities
- Provide feedback and encouragement